T0146397

# POWERFUL PRAYERS FOR YOUR FAMILY

## DAVID AND HEATHER KOPP

WATERBROOK
PRESS

POWERFUL PRAYERS FOR YOUR FAMILY
PUBLISHED BY WATERBROOK PRESS
2375 Telstar Drive, Suite 160
Colorado Springs, Colorado 80920
*A division of Random House, Inc.*

Scripture quotations, unless otherwise indicated, are taken from the *Holy Bible, New International Version*®. NIV®. Copyright © 1973, 1978, 1984 by International Bible Society. Used by permission of Zondervan Publishing House. All rights reserved. Scripture quotations marked (TLB) are taken from *The Living Bible* copyright © 1971. Used by permission of Tyndale House Publishers, Inc., Wheaton, Illinois 60189. All rights reserved. Scripture quotations marked (Phillips) are taken from *The New Testament in Modern English, Revised Edition* © 1972 by J. B. Phillips. Scripture quotations marked (KJV) are taken from the *King James Version*. Scripture quotations marked (NASB) are taken from the *New American Standard Bible*®. © Copyright The Lockman Foundation 1960, 1962, 1963, 1968, 1971, 1972, 1973, 1975, 1977. Used by permission. (www.Lockman.org) Scripture quotations marked (NKJV) are taken from the *New King James Version.* Copyright © 1982 by Thomas Nelson, Inc. Used by permission. All rights reserved. Scripture quotations marked (NLT) are taken from the *Holy Bible, New Living Translation,* copyright © 1996. Used by permission of Tyndale House Publishers, Inc., Wheaton, Illinois 60189. All rights reserved. Scripture quotations marked (RSV) are taken from the *Revised Standard Version of the Bible,* copyright © 1946, 1952, and 1971 by the Division of Christian Education of the National Council of the Churches of Christ in the USA. Used by permission. Scripture quotations marked (NCV) are taken from *The Holy Bible, New Century Version,* copyright © 1987, 1988, 1991 by Word Publishing, Nashville, TN 37214. Used by permission. Scripture quotations marked (ICB) are taken from the *International Children's Bible, New Century Version* ©1986, 1988 by Word Publishing, Nashville, TN 37214. Used by permission. Scripture quotations marked (TEV) are from the *Today's English Version* —Second Edition. Copyright © 1992 by American Bible Society. Used by permission.

ISBN 1-57856-853-6
ISBN-13: 978-1-578-56853-6

Copyright © 2000 by David and Heather Kopp

Previously published under the title *Praying the Bible With Your Family,* copyright © 2000 by David and Heather Kopp.

All rights reserved. No part of this book may be reproduced or transmitted in any form or by any means, electronic or mechanical, including photocopying and recording, or by any information storage and retrieval system, without permission in writing from the publisher.

WATERBROOK and its deer design logo are registered trademarks of WaterBrook Press, a division of Random House, Inc.

The Library of Congress has cataloged the original edition as follows:

Kopp, David, 1949-

    Praying the Bible with your family / David and Heather Kopp.
      p. cm.
    Includes index.
    ISBN 1-57856-384-4
      1. Family—Prayer-books and devotions—English. 2. Bible—Devotional use. I. Kopp, Heather Harpham, 1964- II. Title.
    BV255 .K66 2000
    249—dc21

                                        00-033373

Printed in the United States of America
2004

# Contents

Foreword by Bruce Wilkinson
iv

O N E

The Family That Prays Together...
1

T W O

Daily Prayers
15

T H R E E

Prayers for Special Times
197

F O U R

Indexes
211

# Foreword

I wonder what deep needs you and your family face today. You may be looking for answers to pressing financial or health concerns. You may have a child or loved one who needs a spiritual awakening. Your marriage may need a fresh wind of understanding, forgiveness, and love. You may want to personally experience more of the nearness of Christ in your daily life.

Friend, your prayers are *meant* to make great things happen. And the very fact that you're holding this book and reading this page tells me that you are about to experience more truth and power, more answers to prayer for yourself and those you love than ever before.

Why would I think that, you wonder?

Because picking up this book indicates something extremely important about you, I believe. It strongly suggests that you are ready to take God at His Word and expect life-changing answers when you pray.

As surprising as it may sound, that desire sets you apart from many believers today. In fact, it's been my observation that millions of contemporary Christians really, honestly *don't* believe that prayer is meant to change things in a big way. They might concede that prayer can help your emotional state or give you more spiritual enlightenment. But prayer that results in observable, even miraculous, answers for us, our families, and our world on a *regular* basis? That kind of belief seems naïve to them, or too self-centered, or just too good to be true.

Interestingly, Jesus Himself made the most astonishing statements in the whole Bible about prayer. For example, He said, "If you abide in Me, and My words abide in you, you will ask what you desire, and it shall be done for you" (John 15:7, NKJV).

As a follower of Jesus, I believe prayer that expects answers is simply faith at work. And faith always begins with taking God at His Word.

Approximately three thousand years ago, one of history's great nobodies decided to take God at His Word. His name was Jabez. When he looked at himself and his circumstances, he saw no reason to hope, no opportunity for change, and certainly no sign that a miracle might be in store. Yet he prayed a simple, bold prayer that is still changing lives today. You can read his mini-biography and his request in 1 Chronicles 4:9-10. Here is what Jabez prayed, according to the *New King James* translation:

> "Oh that You would bless me indeed, and enlarge my territory, that Your hand would be with me, and that You would keep me from evil, that I may not cause pain!"

The next sentence records what happened:

> "So God granted him what he requested."

Talk about results! Each of his four requests brought Jabez answers from God, honor in his generation, and an impact among millions who are still learning from his example.

Obviously, how we pray *does* make a difference, and there's much to be learned from Jabez's prayer. But right now I want you to notice one thing in particular: *Jabez desperately wanted to receive what God was waiting to give.*

Let me show you what I mean:

- Jabez cried out for more blessing. God had already promised to bless Abraham and his descendants, and the whole world through them. (See Genesis 12:1-3.)
- Jabez begged for more territory. God had already commanded Moses to conquer and fully occupy all the lands He had given to Israel. (See Deuteronomy 1:8.)
- Jabez pleaded for more of God's power. God had already promised Joshua His presence and power. (See Joshua 1:1-9.)

- And Jabez called out to God for protection from sin and evil. God had already revealed to Israel the choice between "life and good, death and evil" and how to live if they wanted to receive His blessing and protection. (See Deuteronomy 30:15-16.)

It's quite possible that the reason God granted Jabez's requests was that, long after others in Israel had stop expecting very much from God, Jabez still wanted—and asked for—all that God in His goodness had promised!

I've heard from thousands of modern-day Jabezes who are seeing extraordinary results as they pray this scriptural prayer. Not because the words are in any way magical, mind you, but because these individuals are wholeheartedly asking—perhaps for the first time—for God's answers in God's way.

That's where the Powerful Prayers series can help you. Carefully, conscientiously, and expectantly praying Scripture is one way we can know that, as Paul said, we "have the mind of Christ" (1 Corinthians 2:16). Written by my good friends and coworkers David and Heather Kopp, these honest and personal prayers can help you hear God's heart while expressing the deepest desires of your own.

If you're ready to know God better and ask for His very best, this book is for you. I highly recommend it.

May God bless you as you reach for a larger life for His glory and expect greater blessings from Him than you have ever imagined before. Your God is that good, and that ready to answer.

—BRUCE WILKINSON, author, *The Prayer of Jabez*

# The Family That
# Prays Together...

# The Family That Prays Together...

Two yellowing squares of notepaper have stayed in my Bible over the years. I (David) use them for bookmarks. And quite honestly, I lose them somewhere in Leviticus or Habakkuk for years at a time. But even when they're forgotten, they stay in the order they should be read.

The first note, penciled in the fat print and broken lines of a second grader, reads:

> to dad
> I love
> you do
> you love
> me?
> yes/no

There's a check mark over the "yes."
The second note reads:

> me the
> same Jana
> to dad

Since you're a parent, you can probably identify with the feelings that are attached to those mementos. I can remember the exact row in church where we sat as my daughter pulled on a long, blond braid and spelled out the letters of her correspondence. But over the years (Jana is in high school now), those notes in all their simplicity and yearning have come to remind me about the central message of the Bible they nestle in. From the first humans in the garden to first-century Christians in jail, you can hear God's people crying out the same question. And every page of the Bible answers with a check mark over the "yes."

God's Word is a Father's note passed to you and me: "I love you. Do you love me? Yes/No." Then He watches to see on which word our pencil will land.

Real, living prayer in a family starts with the same question of the heart. After all, our children can be taught to recite most anything. We can be diligent about teaching the meaning and purpose of prayer, and faithful in trying to help our kids develop their own prayer habits. We might even succeed at praying with such amazing authority and conviction in their presence that they'll never forget it. But prayer as a conversation that they'll pursue on their own with God still begins with that question of the heart. Love—yes or no?

Think of *Praying the Bible with Your Family* as a daily encouragement for you and your children just to open the Bible and listen. Assume, for example, that this Holy Book is more than history or theology—it's a letter to dads and moms and children. Cherish it as handwritten and very personal. Receive it as the answering Voice that can turn praying from talking into the air into a two-way conversation between child and Father, Father and child.

## GOD'S PRAYER BOOK

The Bible is a ready-made prayer book for God's family. In fact, many passages are recorded prayers, the best-loved being the Psalms. For more than three thousand years, believers have used the Psalms as a prayer book for private and public worship. And at the heart of the book is the 119th Psalm—176 verses of "praying Scripture"!

We "pray the Bible" when we use passages of Scripture to form prayers or when we say the verses directly back to God, making them our own petitions. Jesus said, "If you remain in me and my words remain in you, ask whatever you wish, and it will be given you" (John 15:7).

Moses used God's own words to intercede for his stubborn mob of desert wanderers. Jesus often used scripture in His prayers for Himself and His disciples. In fact, throughout the Bible, we see examples of godly men and women incorporating God's promises and commands in their petitions to Him. They used the Word in their prayers for encouragement, calling to mind who God is and what He has done. Jesus and His disciples sang the psalms together as part of morning and evening prayers. And at the moment of His greatest agony on the cross, Jesus cried out the words of a psalm: "My God, my God, why have you forsaken me?" (Ps. 22:1).

In our family the heritage of Bible praying traces back to my father, Joe Kopp. He grew up with a zeal for memorizing Scripture, partly as a way to overcome a serious speech impediment. But it was a passion that would shape his life and his ministry. When he and my mother went to central Africa as missionaries in 1945, Dad relied on Bible memorization to teach villagers the gospel and help them grow in their faith. And in a very natural way, saying Bible passages back to God became part of his church services and of nearly every prayer at home, too. Now when I read certain passages, I can close my eyes and hear Dad's voice praying beside my bed.

And that's the best reason for praying Scripture. In it we hear most clearly our Father's voice.

## WAYS TO PRAY THE BIBLE

If you've written a child's name next to a Bible verse as my mother did for me, and as Heather and I have done for our five children, then you have begun to pray the Bible. You're saying to God, "This is my heart's desire for my child. I agree with the truth and promise of Your words here, and I claim them for my child."

Other ways to pray Scripture with your family include:

- personalizing a Bible prayer

    *Our Father in heaven,*
    Thank You that Jesus showed us and taught us how to talk to You.

    *Hallowed be Your name.*
    We come before You with respect and love today.

- personalizing a Bible teaching

    Thank You, Father, for never being too busy or making us wait while You listen to someone else. Thank You for listening to us when we're happy, grateful, sad, angry, or in any kind of trouble.

    Your Word says, *Call upon me in the day of trouble; I will deliver you, and you will honor me* (Ps. 50:15).

- praying through a Bible passage

    Dear Great Shepherd, yes, You are this family's Shepherd. Because of this, we know we'll never be without anything we truly need (Ps. 23:1).

    or,

    Whatever we do, help us to work at it with all our heart, as working for the Lord, not for men, since we know that we will receive an inheritance from the Lord as our reward. It is the Lord Christ we are serving (from Col. 3:23-24)!

- personalizing a Bible promise

Help us to keep asking for big, big things because:
*You can do more than we ask or imagine!* (Eph. 3:20).
We know that even now a miracle might be knock-
ing on our door.
*You can do more than we ask or imagine!*

• personalizing a Bible story

[Zacchaeus encounters Jesus]
Thank You, Lord Jesus, that You are willing to go out
of Your way to look for people who are looking for You
(Luke 19:5).
or,
[Daniel in the lions' den]
Thank You, almighty God! You promise to protect us
as You did Daniel: *I will command my angels concerning
you to guard you in all your ways* (Ps. 91:11).

• personalizing a Bible statement as a response from God

Thank You that when I make a mistake and fall into sin,
You look at me and see the goodness of Jesus, and You
say, *Oh, how beautiful you are...!* (Song of Songs 4:1).
or,
Today we want to remember and claim these "great and
precious promises" for our family: *Everyone who receives
me and believes in my name becomes a child of God* (from
John 1:12).

• personalizing a Bible truth as a meditation

I am welcome in my Father's presence today—no matter
what (Heb. 10:19-22).

# BENEFITS OF PRAYING THE BIBLE

Here are some ways that praying Scripture has enriched the devotional experience of families like yours:

*Praying the Bible gets us "unstuck."* Ever listened to yourself praying by your child's bed and thought, "I've been saying these same sentences in the same order for weeks"? Sometimes we're not motivated to pray because we have a record of mediocre experiences with it—we get distracted, bored, vague. Words and ideas fail us.

Praying intentionally with Scripture in mind is like choosing to follow a map in new territory. Suddenly you can spot several worthy destinations. You can pray confidently and specifically: "Thank You, God, that as Brooke makes You Lord of her future, You'll show her step by step how to make the right decisions" (Prov. 3:6).

*Praying the Bible helps us get our memory back.* Sometimes we feel so overwhelmed by feelings and needs that our prayers don't seem to reach beyond the problem. Our kids are no different. We forget God's character, His promises, His past faithfulness and goodness, even His extravagances with us. Praying the truths of the Bible helps us remember what God has done, and what He can still do.

Jeremiah was an emotional priest called to speak for God during the siege and fall of Jerusalem. When he focused on the terrors around him, Jeremiah felt personally assaulted, even abandoned by God: "He pierced my heart with arrows from his quiver" (Lam. 3:13). Only when he focused on God's past mercies did he find strength and encouragement: "Yet this I call to mind and therefore I have hope: Because of the Lord's great love we are not consumed, for his compassions never fail" (3:21-22).

*Praying the Bible helps us pray confidently and expectantly because we're praying in line with God's will.* Heather and I still smile when we remember Nathan's distracted prayer one day. It went something like "I hope

8

everyone here has a good day, and I hope I do well in basketball. Amen." When he was done, we had a lively conversation about that word, "hope." Praying is more than making a wish, we said. We come face to face with God, ask Him to do something, and *know* we're heard.

Without intending to, we can pray ignorantly, even at cross-purposes with what God wants. Jesus told the Pharisees, "You are in error because you do not know the Scriptures or the power of God" (Matt. 22:29). In the same way we use the Bible to measure the content of a sermon or lesson, we can use Scripture to test our motives and reveal the big picture in prayer. When a child prays the Bible back to God, he or she is speaking to God in the words of God with the truth of God. And God promises to answer (1 John 5:14).

Wayne Spear writes that faith is not a belief that "anything can happen," but a confidence that what God has promised *will* happen.[1] When families purposefully pray in harmony with the principles of Scripture, we can be sure that our needs will be met even though we leave the how and when to God.

*Praying the Bible helps our family nurture a growing relationship with God.* Imagine how confused a fiancée would get about her husband-to-be's affections for her if she never opened her mail from him or answered his phone calls. In the same way, when we only bring our changing moods and immediate felt needs into our prayer conversation, we can get just as confused about who God is and what is possible. Our spiritual relationship can start to flounder and cool.

But for us and our kids, Bible-centered praying can lead us into an encounter with the Father-heart of God. An anxious, lonely child can hear her heavenly Father's voice saying to her: "Fear not, for I have redeemed you; I have called you by name, you are mine" (Isa. 43:1-2, RSV). And, perhaps for the first time, she can understand her faith as a relationship as well as a set of beliefs—and begin to truly look forward to her prayer experience.

## What Praying the Bible Doesn't Mean

Praying the Bible doesn't mean ordinary families have to leave out the messy truth about our humanness when we talk with God. Consider how many of David's psalms begin with an unrestrained cry from the depths. How freeing it is to know that God longs for honest communication with His children! Unlike the cashier at the grocery store, when God asks, "How are you today?" He really wants to know. We and our children can approach Him confidently, sure that He hears us with grace regardless of our faults (Heb. 10:19-22).

It's a good thing for our family that praying the Bible is not about using fancy language or sounding religious either. In Matthew 6, Jesus warned about praying aloud just to look more "spiritual" to others. He said that bombarding God with excess words in hopes that He will hear you better indicates a lack of faith, not more of it. We don't need to "talk better" to be acceptable to God. Nor can we manipulate or impress Him with our carefully crafted prayers. The true test of our praying lies in our simple faith, the intention behind our words, and a pure devotion to God's will.

Neither does praying the Bible mean that we always get what we want. In fact, you may want to talk with your children about the difference between praying with faith and praying with magic. We pray "magically" when we believe that a certain arrangement of words, like the right coins inserted in a vending machine, will guarantee the same result every time. Even adults who've been Christians for years can still slip into this mistake. It's true that we have access to power in Jesus' name, that we receive power through God's Word, and that we can release God's power through our faith. But we can't control God's actions, no matter how we pray. Our fallen world comes complete with chaos, tragedy, uncertainty, and personal trials of all kinds. Jesus' promise to us is not that we can magically escape them but that with His help we can overcome them (John 16:33).

## How to Use This Book

In the prayers that follow, you'll find Scripture-based prayers in a variety of formats. Any of these prayers can be read aloud by one person, perhaps taking turns on who is the designated "reader." Most prayers are suitable for anyone in the family to pray. Some are simpler than others to give opportunities for younger family members to participate. And we've tried to offer other family-involving ways to read these prayers. Here are some examples:

*Stanza prayers.* These are prayers with short lines that work well as a leader reads each line and then the rest of the family repeats it. Often the length is short and the wording is simple, making these prayers great practice for young readers.

*Refrain prayers.* These prayers are similar to stanza prayers in that there is a leader and the family repeats. However, the lines are longer, and the line repeated by the family is always the same refrain. For example, when praying through the story of David and Goliath (see page 141), the repeated line is "The battle is the Lord's!" The leader should review the refrain with the family before beginning to pray.

*Meditation prayers.* These are short restatements of scriptures which are meant to be read aloud and then repeated throughout the day. Most are brief enough to memorize easily or to slip into a briefcase, backpack, or handbag.

References in the text always point the way to the Bible passage at hand. The words of the Bible are used as is or modified slightly for personal application, or the prayer addresses a given passage or collection of verses.

In an effort to make *Praying the Bible with Your Family* a complete devotional experience, we've also added other elements we hope your family will enjoy:

- The scripture for the day is followed by explanatory or devotional thoughts. Reading through this together or summarizing it for your family will help you and your children to focus on the text and theme at hand.

- In "Family Talk" you'll find questions to help you and your children have a fun and stimulating discussion about key issues raised by the scripture and devotional and how they relate to your family.

- A Bible knowledge question related to the passage and ranging from easy to difficult will bring out your kids' competitive spirit and get them thumbing through their Bibles.

- After the "Praying the Bible Together" prayer, an easy-to-remember "Truth to Go" will give even your youngest children something to take with them through the day. We encourage kids to write these down in the notebook they'll be taking to school, and parents to slip them as reminders into school lunches or backpacks.

We encourage you to keep *Praying the Bible for Your Family* near your kitchen table or on the coffee table and use it as part of your regular devotional time. Use the title and topical indexes to help you track down a prayer that meets a specific need. Heather and I have tried to write prayers that will represent a range of common family concerns, such as character traits, protection and deliverance, wisdom and guidance, emotional and relationship needs, blessing and provision, thanks and praise, confession, intercession for others, spiritual growth and Christian living, and intimacy with God.

Our hope is that these written prayers will become your own heartfelt expressions. Most of all, we hope you experience these prayers as a personal invitation from the Father—notes to be found, read, and treasured. A fresh way for you and your children to say, "Yes, I love you!" to God, and to hear Him say, "Me the same" in return.

Here's our prayer for you...

*Heavenly Father,*

*In Jesus' name, we pray—and are confident—that You will give endurance, encouragement, and hope to the family that is about to use these pages in conversation with You (Rom. 15:5,13). We thank You, Lord, that You will accomplish immeasurably more than all we could ask or imagine for this praying family (Eph. 3:20). Thank You so much that You want to be known by Your children, and that You lend us Your own resurrection power to help make it happen (Ps. 25:14; 1 Pet. 1:21).*

*Please, Lord, teach our families to pray! Answer every prayer for this family's extravagant good, as only You can (Luke 11:1; 1 John 5:14-15; Rom. 8:28). May Your living words, Your indescribable peace, and Your awesome presence flourish in their lives for all to see (Col. 3:15-16).*

*How good it is to seek You and to wait for Your reply (Lam. 3:25-26). We love You and praise You! Amen.*

1. Wayne Spear, *The Theology of Prayer* (Grand Rapids: Baker, 1979), 57.

# Daily Prayers

# 1 | God of Hippos and Hailstones

*The LORD answered Job out of the storm.... "Brace yourself like a man; I will question you, and you shall answer me. Where were you when I laid the earth's foundation? Tell me, if you understand. Who marked off its dimensions? Surely you know! Who stretched a measuring line across it?"*

JOB 38:1,4-5

The book of Job is the story of a good man who loves God but who suddenly loses everything—his children, his money, and his health. Now that he's miserable, will he still love God? Satan is counting on Job to say, "No way!"

But Job hangs on. "Even if God kills me, I'll still trust him," he tells his friends (from 13:15). What he wants most, he says, is to talk to God face to face.

Finally God arrives in a storm to answer Job. But instead of explaining why bad things happen, God says, "Look at my wonderful creation! Isn't it something? Do you have *any idea* how I did that?" For the next four chapters, God talks about the amazing things He made: stars and oceans, hailstones and thunder, ostriches, whales, and hippopotamuses...

"Look! Look! Look!" God seems to say to his friend Job. "Can't you see I'm a big enough God for you—even when bad things happen?"

### FAMILY TALK

⇝ What do you think is the most amazing thing God made?

⇝ What does it tell you about God's character?

### "WHERE WERE YOU?"

Scientists like to argue about how the world was made. Who was the only one who actually saw it happen? (Gen. 1)

# Praying the Bible Together

God of hippopotamuses and hailstones, Lord of rainbows and coconut trees, Maker of snowflakes and snails and parakeets, Father of every living person—especially in this house...

We worship You today! Our family praises You for Your love and strength! We thank You for this beautiful world You've made. Your creative genius makes even the smartest human seem about as smart as a rock.

Lord, we want to begin where the Bible begins. Your Word says, "In the beginning, God created..." (Gen. 1:1). Everything begins with You! When we look at Creation, we can say to You as Job did, "I know that you can do all things" (Job 42:2).

Yes, You can take care of us no matter what happens.

If things go wrong today, help us to be fiercely loyal to You, as Job was. If we feel sad, help us to believe in Your kindness. When people we know get sick, remind us to ask You to make them well soon.

In Your strong name we pray. Amen.

**TRUTH TO GO**
In the beginning...God created!
(Gen. 1:1)

# 2 | Up a Tree

*A man was there by the name of Zacchaeus; he was a chief tax collector and was wealthy. He wanted to see who Jesus was, but being a short man he could not.... So he ran ahead and climbed a sycamore-fig tree.... When Jesus reached the spot, he looked up and said to him, "Zacchaeus, come down immediately. I must stay at your house today." So he came down at once and welcomed him gladly. All the people saw this and began to mutter, "He has gone to be the guest of a 'sinner.'" But Zacchaeus stood up and said to the Lord, "Look, Lord! Here and now I give half of my possessions to the poor, and if I have cheated anybody out of anything, I will pay back four times the amount." Jesus said to him, "Today salvation has come to this house.... For the Son of Man came to seek and to save what was lost."*

Luke 19:2-10

Zacchaeus was short, sneaky, mean, and very rich. In Roman times tax collectors were traitors and crooks. They collected more than what was owed and kept the extra for themselves. No wonder nobody wanted to let Zacchaeus in front to see Jesus! But Jesus knew a secret: Zacchaeus wanted to start over. In fact, Jesus said Zacchaeus was just the kind of person He had come to save!

### FAMILY TALK

➤ How could you surprise a "Zacchaeus" you know with the good news of Jesus?

### SHORT AND SHORTER

Zacchaeus is the shortest man in the Bible. What is the shortest book? (Hint: It's in the New Testament and has only thirteen verses.)

# Praying the Bible Together

Thank You, Lord Jesus,
that You are willing to go out of Your way
to look for people
who are looking for You.

Thank You that You came
not just for good people,
but for all kinds of losers
and cheaters
and liars.
Your saving love, O Lord, is awesome!

Show us someone who is searching for You
but is stuck up a tree.
Help us to smile and say, "Hello,"
and invite him down to meet You.
Amen.

**TRUTH TO GO**
Jesus is looking for people who are lost.
(Luke 19:10)

# 3 | A Jesus Kind of Love

*Let us not love with words or tongue, but with actions and in truth. We love because [He] first loved us.*

1 JOHN 3:18; 4:19

When you love someone, what's supposed to happen? According to the movies, you feel warm and fizzy and dizzy inside when a certain special person is around. The Bible talks about this kind of love, too (it's called romantic love). But the Bible talks more about another kind of love.

It's not feeling fizzy or dizzy. In fact it's not really about feelings at all. This kind of love is wise and strong enough to help you do things you would rather not do. Like be kind to a mean neighbor. Or clean up a mess you didn't make. Jesus said the very best kind of love is so strong, you can even love your enemies (Matt. 5:44).

Jesus didn't mean you should have nice feelings about people who hurt you. He was talking about the words and actions you choose in all your relationships. A Jesus kind of love is about what you do, not what you feel.

### FAMILY TALK

↬ Name someone you find especially hard to *feel* love toward. Then think of one thing you could *do* that would show a Jesus kind of love.

### HARD LOVE

What did Jesus do for the men who crucified Him? (Luke 23:34)

# Praying the Bible Together

Dear Lord Jesus,
Show our family how to love each other
by what we do and by what we say—
no matter how we feel.
Help us to love each other at all times,
even when it feels hard.

Jesus, You ask us to do good to our enemies
and bless them.
We want to obey You.
You loved the whole human race
while we still hated You
and ran away from Your love (Rom. 5:8).
You forgave those who crucified You (Luke 23:34).
You rose again for those who betrayed You
    (Acts 2:23-24).
Fill our hearts and change our actions
by this Jesus kind of love today.
Amen.

**TRUTH TO GO**
In our family, love is an *action* word.
(from 1 John 3:18)

# 4 | There's a Frog in My Bed! There's a Frog on My Head!

*Then the LORD said to Moses, "Go to Pharaoh and say to him, 'This is what the LORD says: Let my people go, so that they may worship me. If you refuse to let them go, I will plague your whole country with frogs....'" Then the LORD said to Moses, "Tell Aaron, 'Stretch out your hand with your staff over the streams and canals and ponds, and make frogs come up on the land of Egypt.'" So Aaron stretched out his hand over the waters of Egypt, and the frogs came up and covered the land.*

EXODUS 8:1-6

Pharaoh, king of Egypt, was treating God's people like slaves. But when Moses asked for their freedom, Pharaoh refused to let the Jews go. So God sent some hopping, croaking, slippery trouble his way.

"Let my people go!" Moses demanded. His words have become the cry of freedom for African Americans and many other oppressed peoples through the centuries. God wants all people to be free so that we can live with dignity and worship Him with what we say and do.

### FAMILY TALK

- One meaning of "plague" is too many of the wrong things taking over your life. Is your family suffering from a plague these days (too many activities, too much TV, too much quarreling)?
- Egyptians worshiped the Nile River. What do you think God was trying to tell them when their idol brought them nothing but frogs?

### CROCODILE SEZ...
On which continent is the Nile River? (Isa. 23:10, NCV)

# Praying the Bible Together

Dear Lord,

Show us if our lives are getting overrun by a plague of silly things, busy things, or even dangerous things.

Lord, keep us free from the frog of worry. The Bible says, "Do not be anxious about anything" (Phil. 4:6).

Lord, keep us free from the frogs of envying other people or wanting what they have. Your Word says, "Rid yourselves of all...envy" (1 Pet. 2:1) and "You shall not covet" (Exod. 20:17).

Lord, keep us free from the frogs of so much noise and busyness that we can't hear Your Holy Spirit. Your Word says, "Be still, and know that I am God" (Ps. 46:10).

Lord, keep us free from the plague of loving money. The Bible says, "People who want to get rich fall into temptation and a trap" (1 Tim. 6:9).

Lord, keep us free from any habits, influences, or people that might destroy our bodies or our spirits. Your Word says, "A man is a slave to whatever has mastered him" (2 Pet. 2:19).

Thank You for setting us free from plagues of every kind. Help each of us to stand firm today, and not get dragged back into slavery of any kind. May we use our freedom to serve You and others (Gal. 5:1).

In Jesus' name. Amen.

**TRUTH TO GO**
Jesus sets me free.
(John 8:36)

# 5 | A Champion Giver

*But just as you excel in everything—in faith, in speech, in knowledge, in complete earnestness and in your love for us—see that you also excel in this grace of giving.*

2 CORINTHIANS 8:7

The Christians in a city called Corinth seemed to take most of the prizes. They were richer, smarter, and more educated. Paul said they even talked better! But they were forgetting something important. Paul urged them, "Try to be number one in giving, too!"

Giving means we offer our belongings to someone who needs them. We can give to a person, a church, or an organization that helps the hungry or the homeless. God uses what we give to make good things happen for others.

Are you a champion giver? The Bible says we are to give more than just the extra we might have lying around (Luke 21:2-4) and give cheerfully (2 Cor. 9:7). Then we'll excel at "this grace of giving."

### FAMILY TALK

Acts 20:35 says, "It is more blessed to give than to receive." Can you remember a time when you gave generously to someone—and felt that you benefited even more than the person you gave to?

### MISERS

Who lied about giving to a church—and died as a result?
(Acts 5:1-11)

# Praying the Bible Together

Heavenly Father,
Teach us today
how to be good at giving
because "It is better to give than to receive"
    (from Acts 20:35).

We want to give a lot
and with a cheerful spirit
so others will be happy to receive
because "the Lord loves a cheerful giver"
    (from 2 Cor. 9:7).

Help us to give even if it hurts a little,
even if we might miss what we gave away,
because You loved the world so much
that You gave us eternal life
when it cost You everything
—even Your own Son (John 3:16).
Amen.

**TRUTH TO GO**
God loves a cheerful giver.
(2 Cor. 9:7)

# 6 | Mouth on Fire

*When we put bits into the mouths of horses to make them obey us, we can turn the whole animal. Or take ships as an example. Although they are so large and are driven by strong winds, they are steered by a very small rudder wherever the pilot wants to go. Likewise the tongue is a small part of the body, but it makes great boasts. Consider what a great forest is set on fire by a small spark. The tongue is also a fire, a world of evil among the parts of the body.*

JAMES 3:3-6

When your teacher wants to make an important point, she says it more than once. James really wanted Christians to understand the power of words. So he gave three different word pictures of what can happen if we don't control them: Your tongue can be like a horse running wild with no bridle to control it; your tongue can be like a ship with a broken rudder, adrift in a storm; your tongue can be like a spark that starts a forest fire. Small things, like criticism or unkind remarks, can lead to a lot of trouble and hurt.

### FAMILY TALK

➤ Are there "tongue traps" your family needs to work on (e.g., critical remarks, negative talk, interrupting, speaking without thinking first)?

### "AND GOD ... "?

Did God begin each Creation day with a word or an action? (Gen. 1)

# Praying the Bible Together

Lord,
Help us all watch our words today.
We're sorry that sometimes we say the wrong thing.
Please forgive us.
You made words so powerful!
Help us to use that power
to encourage,
to praise,
to be thankful,
to be helpful,
to be kind,
and to say Your name with respect.

Help us to slow down and think before we talk.
We don't want to start a fire
when we could have sparked a smile.
We pray in Jesus' name. Amen.

**TRUTH TO GO**
What I say has power to help or to hurt.
(from James 3:5)

# 7 | Oh No, Not Manna Again!

*The rabble with them began to crave other food, and again the Israelites started wailing and said, "If only we had meat to eat!... We never see anything but this manna!"*

NUMBERS 11:4-6

Once when the Israelites were wandering in desert country for forty years, they got hungry and complained to God. He rained down special food for them to eat every day. It was called manna, it tasted like honey, it was free, and all they had to do was pick it up off the ground every morning—for forty years!

After a while the Israelites got tired of eating the same thing over and over, and they started complaining again. Then God sent quail for them to eat. God didn't mind that His people wanted a variety of things to eat. But their grumbling and complaining made Him angry.

When we focus on what we don't have, we stop being grateful for what we do have. "Give thanks in all circumstances," wrote Paul, "for this is God's will for you in Christ Jesus" (1 Thess. 5:18).

Remember: God will *always* take care of us. That's why He asks for gratitude, not a lousy attitude!

## FAMILY TALK

- What have you complained about lately?
- Name three good things God has done that you could be more grateful for.

## FOOD FOR THOUGHT

What four young men in the Old Testament were known for cheerfully eating all their vegetables? (Dan. 1:11-12)

# Praying the Bible Together

Dear God,

It's so easy for us to forget all the good things we have.
Today we choose gratitude instead of a lousy attitude.
Help us to...

*Give thanks in every circumstance* (1 Thess. 5:18)!
Please forgive us for focusing on what we don't have.
Today we want to be happy and content.
Help us to...

*Give thanks in every circumstance!*
It's easy for us to get bored or cranky or impatient.
But today we trust that You're always at work.
So help us to...

*Give thanks in every circumstance!*
It's easy for us to think only about our little plans.
Today we don't want to miss Your plans for us.
Help us to...

*Give thanks in every circumstance!*
God, You are strong. And You are always with us!
That's why we know it's right to say...

*Give thanks in every circumstance!*
In Jesus' name. Amen.

**TRUTH TO GO**
Have gratitude, not a lousy attitude!
(from 1 Thess. 5:18)

# 8 | Everybody's Special Here

*If you show special attention to the man wearing fine clothes and say, "Here's a good seat for you," but say to the poor man, "You stand there" or "Sit on the floor by my feet," have you not discriminated among yourselves and become judges with evil thoughts?*

JAMES 2:3-4

God doesn't like it when we judge or look down on people just because they're from a different race, place, religion, or social group than we are. In Bible times the Jews called the Gentiles "dogs." Some people called the early Christians "cannibals." That was because they ate the body of Christ (the communion bread) and drank His blood (the communion wine) when they celebrated the Lord's Supper together.

But the Bible teaches that we are all made in the image of God (Gen. 1:26). Jesus came to die for *everyone* (John 3:16). "You are all sons of God," wrote Paul. "There is neither Jew nor Greek, slave nor free, male nor female, for you are all one in Christ Jesus…and heirs according to the promise" (Gal. 3:26,28-29).

### FAMILY TALK

↬ Who do you know that is really different from you? How are they different? How are they like you? How do you feel when you're around them?

↬ How can your family show love to the "different" people you know?

### WRONG SIDE OF THE TRACKS

Even Jesus was discriminated against because He grew up in the "wrong" place. Where was it? (John 1:45-46)

# Praying the Bible Together

Dear Heavenly Father,
Thank You for creating each of us unique,
for making all Your people "different."
Help us not to judge people
because they look different from us,
because their skin is a different color
or their clothes are different
or their body is different
or their voice doesn't sound like ours.
Help me be kind to those
who go to different churches,
and to those who don't go to church at all.
You made everyone with just as much love
as You made me.
Thank You.
In Jesus' name. Amen.

**TRUTH TO GO**
We're all one in Christ.
(Gal. 3:28)

# 9 | Holy Help

*Come to me, all you who are weary and burdened, and I will give you rest.
Take my yoke upon you and learn from me, for I am gentle and humble in
heart, and you will find rest for your souls. For my yoke is easy and my burden is light.*

MATTHEW 11:28-29

Sometimes it seems like such hard work to be a Christian. You can try
as hard as you can to be a kinder person or have a stronger faith, but
you just can't do it! Or at least not for very long.

Think about it: First Jesus told His disciples to be perfect as He was
(Matt. 5:48). Then He said that His burden is easy and His yoke is
light! How can the two statements be in the same book?

God knew that no amount of trying harder could ever make us
completely holy people, worthy of heaven. Only God's grace—offered
free and available to everyone through Jesus—could make us heaven
bound. And His power inside us can make any burden light.

### FAMILY TALK

⟿ What do you think Jesus really meant when He told His disciples to be perfect?

⟿ What does it mean to you to "rest" in Jesus?

### HOLY, HOLY, HOLY

Some Bibles translate "perfect" as "holy." The word "holy"
means to be pure and without sin. In the Old Testament book
of Leviticus, the word "holy" is mentioned eighty-seven times!
Why do you think that is?

# Praying the Bible Together

Most Holy Father,

Why do we try and try to be better people on our own strength? Of course we can't!

You have sent us the Holy Spirit to live in our hearts. And what You have begun in our lives, Lord, only You can complete (Gal. 3:3).

You say if righteousness could be gained through our actions, then Christ died for nothing! (Gal. 2:21). And anyone who thinks human strength or will power will get him to heaven is making a big mistake (Gal. 3:10).

Thank You that You came to earth to show us how to live holy lives that please You. Thank You for bringing us the supernatural power to make it possible.

We pray that You will help us to lean on Your strength today to do what is right. And as we do that, please cover us with Your grace and fill our souls with rest.

Amen.

**TRUTH TO GO**
Live holy by the Holy Spirit.
(Gal. 5:16)

# 10 | Sweet As Honey

*How sweet are your promises to my taste, sweeter than honeycomb to my mouth!*

PSALM 119:103

What's your favorite snack? Ice cream? Pizza? Cookies? In Bible times, honey was everyone's favorite. The psalmists often compared their appetite for God's Word to their craving for honey. They savored God's promises the way you might love the taste of a chocolate chip cookie.

Every single verse of Psalm 119 is a meditation about the appeal of God's Word and the benefits of reading it. For example, the Bible:

- shows you what's valuable and what's not (vv. 36-37)
- tells you about God's love (v. 41)
- brings hope and comfort when things aren't going well (vv. 61,114)
- makes you smarter and helps you make decisions (vv. 105,130)
- makes you happy (v. 111)

What kind of an appetite do you have for the Bible? You can tell by the "snack appeal" test—how often you find yourself reaching to pick it up!

### FAMILY TALK

➤ Write down a Bible verse you especially love, and put it on the fridge. Each time you see it, remember to think about what it means, "tasting" every wonderful word.

### HONEY OVERDOSE

It's impossible to "eat" too much of God's Word. But according to the Bible, what will happen if you eat too much honey? (Prov. 25:16)

# Praying Psalm 119 Together

Lord,
Open our eyes that we may see
    wonderful things in Your Word (v. 18).
Help us to hide Your Word in our hearts
    that we might not sin against You (v. 11).
Your teachings are our delight;
    they are our counselors (v. 24).
Keep us from deceitful ways,
    and cover us with Your grace (v. 29).
Thank You that we can walk around in freedom
    if we seek out Your teachings (v. 45).
You are good, and what You do is good;
    teach us more about You from the Bible (v. 68).
Your Word, O Lord, will last forever;
    it is forever settled in heaven (v. 89).
How sweet are Your promises to our taste,
    yes, sweeter than honey to our mouths! (v. 103).
Amen.

**TRUTH TO GO**
God's Word tastes good.
(Ps. 119:103)

# 11 | A Sterling Reputation

*A good name is more desirable than great riches; to be esteemed is better than silver or gold.*

PROVERBS 22:1

Have you ever met someone who didn't like his or her name? Maybe the name was unique (like Bohanna Pinkerton), or funny (like Rose Bush), or old-fashioned (like Hubert). Some people dislike their names so much that when they grow up they legally change them.

When the Bible talks about a "good name," it's not referring to just the letters or sound of the name. A good name in the Bible means your reputation—what other people think of when they think of you. If you have a good name, that means when people hear it mentioned, they think well of you. They respect who you are and what you have done. They trust you.

The Bible says this kind of good name is worth millions. Even if your name is Dipsy Twinkum!

### FAMILY TALK

➝ In Isaiah 62:2, God promises to give Israel a new name. Some believe that when we get to heaven, God will have a new name for each of us. If you could be all that your name represents, what new name would you like in heaven?

➝ What kind of reputation do you want to have with your friends? Be specific.

### OUCH!
What Bible man was named Pain? (1 Chron. 4:9-10)

# Praying the Bible Together

Dear Lord,

You have said that a good name is worth more than
   silver or gold.

We ask that You would help us to earn a good reputation by what we say and do.

Your Word says:

   "Let love and faithfulness never leave you;

   bind them around your neck,

   write them on the tablet of your heart.

   Then you will win favor and a good name

   in the sight of God and man" (Prov. 3:3-4).

Lord, we really want a family reputation for love and
   faithfulness.

We want to bring praise to You and happiness to
   each other.

Help us make the kind of choices that will
   win favor and respect from others today.

Jesus, You have the name above every name,

and it's in Your name we pray.

Amen.

**TRUTH TO GO**

Keep a good reputation—because you can't lose a bad one.
(Prov. 22:1)

# 12 | The Gift of Laughter

*Sarah said, "God has brought me laughter."*

GENESIS 21:6

Have you ever laughed when you weren't supposed to, and then felt embarrassed? The first time Sarah heard the Lord promise her husband, Abraham, that she was going to get pregnant, she laughed. Why? Because the idea sounded ridiculous! She was ninety years old! But the Lord heard her laugh. When He asked her about it, she was afraid. She said she didn't laugh (Gen. 18:10-15).

A year later she delivered a baby just as the Lord had promised. And the Bible says she laughed again—this time from joy and celebration. In fact she named her baby Isaac, which means "laughter" in Hebrew. She said, "God has brought me laughter, and everyone who hears about this will laugh with me" (Gen. 21:6).

### FAMILY TALK

↪ God didn't have to create laughter. But aren't you glad He did? Share your favorite funny or embarrassing memory.

↪ What's the difference between laughing *at* someone and laughing *with* someone? Give your family a "Laugh Class" report card. "A" means you like to laugh *with* the family. "F" means you usually laugh *at* someone.

### YOU'VE GOT TO BE KIDDING!

Who else laughed at the idea of Sarah's having a baby? (Gen. 17:17)

# Praying the Bible Together

Lord of Laughter,
Thank You so much for the gift of laughter.
We know that You created laughter, so it is a good
  thing,
and You must love to see us laugh with happiness!
We pray that You will give us many reasons to laugh.
Your joy is our strength (Neh. 8:10).
And when we cry, remind us that it's You
who turns mourning into gladness (Jer. 31:13).
Grant us a merry heart that does us good, like medi-
  cine (Prov. 17:22).
May it be said of our family, "They laugh at the days
  to come" (Prov. 31:25)
and find joy in Your presence (Ps. 16:11).
Show us how to find laughter
and bring laughter to others all day.
Because You are our joy.
Amen.

**TRUTH TO GO**
Good laughter is God's medicine.
(Prov. 17:22)

# 13 | Knock Knock

*Ask and it will be given to you; seek and you will find; knock and the door will be opened to you. For everyone who asks receives; he who seeks finds; and to him who knocks, the door will be opened.*

Jesus taught His disciples to be persistent in their prayer requests. Persistence means if you really want something, *keep asking for it!* To show what He meant, Jesus told a story about a poor widow who couldn't get a corrupt judge to listen to her problem and give her help. But the widow wouldn't give up. She kept knocking on his door, pleading for justice. She was such a pest, the judge finally changed his mind. "Even though I don't fear God or care about men," he said, "yet because this widow keeps bothering me, I will see that she gets justice" (Luke 18:4-5).

Pray like that, Jesus said. God will answer. You see, God not only wants us to knock on His door and ask for things, but He invites us to keep asking—and even to "pester" Him!

### FAMILY TALK

↪ Why do you suppose God might want you to keep asking for certain things? Can you think of one thing that you'd like to "pester" God for when you pray? If so, share it with the family, or write it down just for yourself. Then watch for God's answer!

### BEGGING GOD

What Old Testament woman publicly begged God for a child— praying so hard and with such feeling that a priest thought she was drunk? (1 Sam. 1:9-18)

# Praying the Bible Together

Dear Heavenly Father,
Thank You that You aren't like a crooked judge
who says, "Go away! I don't care about you!"
You don't say, "Be quiet. You're a nobody!"
or, "Please, don't bother Me!"
Thank You, dear Lord!
Instead, You are a loving,
listening,
powerful God!
You said, "Ask and it will be given to you."
You said, "Seek and you will find."
You said, "Knock and the door will be opened to you."
Thank You!
Show us what to pray for today
And help us to ask
and ask
and ask again.
Because You've promised to answer.
In Jesus' name. Amen.

**TRUTH TO GO**
If I ask—and keep on asking—God will answer.
(Matt. 7:8)

# 14 | Miracle at the Door

*So Peter was kept in prison, but the church was earnestly praying to God for him.... Peter knocked at the outer entrance, and a servant girl named Rhoda came to answer the door. When she recognized Peter's voice, she was so overjoyed she ran back without opening it and exclaimed, "Peter is at the door!" "You're out of your mind," they told her. When she kept insisting that it was so, they said, "It must be his angel."*

ACTS 12:5,13-15

King Herod had already executed another disciple named James by cutting off his head. Christians were afraid Peter would be next. As Peter's friends prayed for his release from prison, God answered their prayers. But when he showed up at their door one night, they didn't believe it was really him!

Have you ever prayed for something important to happen, then when it did, you were shocked? You didn't really expect God to answer.

### FAMILY TALK

- Maybe the reason Peter's friends didn't believe he was at the door was that they were expecting a different kind of answer. What are some ways you can watch for an answer to your prayers without deciding exactly what the answer should be?
- Come up with one important family need that you can post somewhere and all continue to pray for. Then watch for a surprise!

### "I'M OUTTA HERE!"

Even Peter didn't believe God was getting him out of jail until it was all over. Read about the exciting escape in Acts 12:5-19.

# Praying the Bible Together

Heavenly Father,
Please forgive us for doubting Your promises.
> *You can do more than we ask or imagine!*
(Eph. 3:20).
When we ask You for a miracle, teach us to say:
> *You can do more than we ask or imagine!*
Help us to keep asking for big, big things because
> *You can do more than we ask or imagine!*
Even when our situation looks hopeless,
> *You can do more than we ask or imagine!*
Thank You for being a God who cares.
> *You can do more than we ask or imagine!*
Hear our prayers today, God—even for little things.
> *You can do more than we ask or imagine!*
We know that even now a miracle might be knocking on our door.
> *You can do more than we ask or imagine!*
We believe, Lord! Help us to look for it today!
> Because…
> *You can do more than we ask or imagine!*
In Jesus' name. Amen.

**TRUTH TO GO**
God can do more than I ask or imagine.
(Eph. 3:20)

# 15 | Stop Fighting!

*If you keep on biting and devouring each other, watch out or you will be destroyed by each other.*

GALATIANS 5:15

*Peacemakers who sow in peace raise a harvest of righteousness.*

JAMES 3:18

Have you noticed? People who quarrel a lot only end up hurting each other. Nothing is solved. No one feels better. Everyone loses.

God wants us to be peacemakers. A peacemaker tries to resolve differences in a way that is fair and helpful. Peacemakers don't look for reasons to be right as hard as they look for reasons to say, "Let's get along."

If you plant seeds of peace in your family, God promises to reward you with a harvest of righteousness. A good, everyday definition for "righteousness" is "right choices that lead to an awesome life."

That's why peacemakers are the real winners in a fight!

## FAMILY TALK

- What's the Quarrel Temperature in your house? *Blistering* (we fight all the time). *Plenty hot* (we fight a lot). *Warm* (fights are rare). *Nice and cool* (fights? What fights?)
- Is there one fight that keeps happening? Decide what each of you can do now to improve your record.

## ROYAL REBEL

When Abraham's nephew accused him of taking all the good land, Abraham said, "Take what you want. I'll take what's left." What was the nephew's name? (Gen. 13:1-11)

# Praying the Bible Together

Heavenly Father,

We ask today that our family would make a habit of living at peace with each other. Anything less is a bad idea and doesn't please You. Your Word reminds us that most arguments start from selfish desires (James 4:1). Too often we want what we want, we want it our way, and we want it now!

Forgive us, Father, when we behave that way! We come to You now, God of peace (Heb. 13:20), and humbly ask that Your peace would rule in our hearts (Col. 3:15). The problem isn't that we disagree, but that we attack each other instead of the problem.

Today we ask You to save us from our need to be right, our determination to win, our tendency to punish. We want to forgive each other as freely as You forgive us (Col. 3:13), even when we haven't received the kind of support, understanding, or apology we think we deserve.

Help us to remember Your words: "Do not repay anyone evil for evil. Be careful to do what is right in the eyes of everybody. If it is possible, as far as it depends on you, live at peace with everyone" (Rom. 12:17-18).

Yes, Lord, we want to be peacemakers today. Please help us to work on problems *together* rather than letting them pull us apart.

Amen.

**TRUTH TO GO**
Peacemakers win the most arguments.
(James 3:18)

# 16 | A Family of Aliens

*Dear friends, I urge you, as aliens and strangers in the world, to abstain from sinful desires, which war against your soul. Live such good lives among the pagans that...they may see your good deeds and glorify God.*

1 PETER 2:11-12

In Peter's time, a "pagan" described a person who didn't believe in God or Jesus. When Peter wrote these words, he was asking Christians to set a good example for these nonbelievers.

Today he might put it this way: "Always do the right thing, even if it makes you stand out from the crowd. Even if it makes you feel like a weirdo or an alien! Then people will notice your good deeds, and they'll realize that following Jesus *does* make a difference!"

## FAMILY TALK

↝ Name some good things you could do that would seem "strange" to people who don't follow Jesus.

↝ When is it hardest for you to do these good things?

↝ Are you willing to be a little "strange" for Jesus? Plan your own family Alien Invasion for Jesus—and decide when you'll carry it out.

## ALIEN ENCOUNTER

What prophet lived in the desert, dressed in camel hair, and ate locusts and wild honey? (Matt. 3:1-4)

# Praying the Bible Together

Dear Lord,

We want to be the kind of people who live such good lives that we seem strange sometimes—even like aliens!—to people who don't know You. Lord, we'd rather impress You than a whole crowd of others.

Help us do that today.

Often You ask us to do the complete opposite of what comes naturally.

When we want to pay someone back for a wrong, You tell us: *Love your enemies and pray for those who persecute you* (Matt. 5:44).

When we want to be the one to go first, You tell us: *If anyone wants to be first, he must be the very last, and the servant of all* (Mark 9:35).

When we want to insist on our own way, You tell us: *Think of others as more important than yourselves* (Phil. 2:3).

We are willing to do these things, Lord! But we need the help of Your Holy Spirit showing us how and giving us courage. Help each of us to act exactly as You want us to today.

Then everyone will know that we belong to You!

We pray these things on behalf of our family.

Amen.

**TRUTH TO GO**
God wants me to stand out from the crowd!
(1 Pet. 2:11)

# 17 | The Big Race

*Therefore, since we are surrounded by such a great cloud of witnesses, let us throw off everything that hinders and the sin that so easily entangles, and let us run with perseverance the race marked out for us.*

HEBREWS 12:1

*Run in such a way as to get the prize.*

1 CORINTHIANS 9:24

In Bible times athletic competitions featured many of the same sports as today's Olympic Games—running, boxing, javelin and discus throwing. That's why New Testament writers often compared the Christian life to a sports event.

When the verse says, "Let us throw off everything that hinders," the writer is talking about wrong actions or attitudes that might get in the way of what God wants. You wouldn't run a race in your boots, would you? No, you strip down to just the basics so you can run as fast as possible (Greek athletes sometimes ran naked!).

After all, God Himself is cheering you on. And with His help, you can win!

### FAMILY TALK

↪ How are being a Christian and running a race similar?

↪ How do you feel you are running lately? Ask God to show you what action or attitude or value you might need to throw away so you can win the race.

### SPORTS IN ISRAEL
What sport did Saul's son Jonathan practice? (1 Sam. 20:20)

# Praying the Bible Together

Dear Lord,
We know we are in a race today.
Please help us to live for You—
and run to win first place.
Thank You that we are cheered on by a great crowd
  of Christians
who watch us from heaven.
Today we choose to toss aside anything
that might slow us down
or get us off track.
Help us to get rid of weights
like laziness or selfishness,
like anger or pride.
Then we will be able to run and win
the race You have marked out for us.
Amen.

**TRUTH TO GO**
If I run to get the prize—I'll win.
(1 Cor. 9:24)

# 18 | Angels Welcome Here

*Do not neglect to show hospitality to strangers, for by this some have entertained angels without knowing it.*

HEBREWS 13:2, NASB

*Offer hospitality to one another without grumbling.*

1 PETER 4:9

When was the last time you showed hospitality to someone you didn't know? Hospitality doesn't necessarily have to mean you offer someone food and shelter. Anytime you offer a kindness to a stranger, you are doing what God asks. Hospitality is making others feel at home. When Paul taught the Roman believers to practice hospitality (Rom. 12:13), the Greek word he used meant "to love strangers."

Abraham once entertained three strangers who turned out to be angels. Next time you cross paths with a stranger in need, remember that it might really be an angel!

### FAMILY TALK

↬ An old Oriental proverb says, "Every stranger is an invited guest." What do you think this means?

↬ How might you act differently toward strangers if you really thought they were angels?

### DUMBSTRUCK

Which New Testament man lost his voice after he doubted the message of an angel? (Luke 1:18–20)

# Praying the Bible Together

Lord,
Today we pray that You would teach all of us
what it means to offer hospitality.
Please send angels to our house,
knowing that we won't send them away.
Help us treat strangers with wisdom and caution—
in case they are dangerous;
but also with kindness and care—
in case they are angels in disguise!
Help us work together happily
to make anyone who comes to stay with us
    comfortable.
May our house be like Your house, Lord:
cozy and welcoming,
a place where friends, strangers—and angels—
feel like part of the family.
Amen.

**TRUTH TO GO**
Home is the kindest gift.
(Heb. 13:2)

# 19 | A Humble Outfit

*All of you, clothe yourselves with humility toward one another, because, "God opposes the proud but gives grace to the humble."*

1 PETER 5:5

These days, we hear a lot of talk about the need for confidence and good self-esteem. Jesus reminds us that true self-esteem doesn't come from having pride in ourselves but from being humble. We're humble when we don't boast about being better than everyone else. It's not wrong to have confidence in our abilities and strengths. But we didn't create them; God did.

Be careful, Peter says in this verse, because the wrong kind of pride can cause God to actually oppose you! So remember, put on humility every morning when you get dressed. Then God will be *for* you all day long!

### FAMILY TALK

- Paul told the Corinthians that knowledge—or pride—"puffs up" but love "builds up" (1 Cor. 8:1). Have you ever seen someone "puffed up" about themselves? How did they act?
- Look up Romans 12:3, and then talk about the difference between "bad" pride and "good" pride.

### HUMBLE PIE

Can you fill in the blank? (Hint: The speaker is Moses.) "He gave you _____ to eat in the desert, something your fathers had never known, to humble and to test you so that in the end it might go well with you." (Deut. 8:16)

# Praying the Bible Together

Lord Jesus,

Teach our family about humility, we pray. It's so easy to be arrogant and not even know it. But the Bible says the Lord "guides the humble in what is right and teaches them his way" (Ps. 25:9). That's what we pray for today.

Show us the difference between thinking too much of ourselves and seeing ourselves accurately (Rom. 12:3). Teach us to love the praise of God more than the praise of men (John 12:43).

We know that if we are stuck-up rather than humble, we will run into all kinds of trouble (Prov. 16:18). Help our whole family to remember that if we are willing to take the lower position, then You will personally lift us up (James 4:10). And show us how to put the power of humility to work with our friends, at school, in sports, and at church.

What gifts do any of us have that You did not give us? Thank You for all the gifts and abilities You've given us. Now I pray that as we put away pride and selfishness, You will shine through our words and actions and get all the credit (James 1:17).

Amen.

**TRUTH TO GO**
I make God proud when I wear humility.
(1 Pet. 5:5)

# 20 | "Speak, Lord—I'm Listening…"

*Then Eli realized that the LORD was calling the boy. So Eli told Samuel, "Go and lie down, and if he calls you, say, 'Speak, LORD for your servant is listening.'" So Samuel went and lay down in his place. The LORD came and stood there, calling as at the other times, "Samuel! Samuel!" Then Samuel said, "Speak, for your servant is listening."*

1 SAMUEL 3:8-10

Samuel's mother had promised that if God gave her a son, she would let him grow up in the temple so he could learn to be a priest and serve God his whole life. One night while little Samuel was lying in bed, he kept hearing a voice calling his name. At first he thought it was the priest. But it turned out to be God talking to him. As Samuel grew up, he kept listening carefully to what God was saying to him, and he became a great prophet.

## FAMILY TALK

↬ The Bible describes the voice of God as very quiet (1 Kings 19:12) but promises that every child of God can hear it (John 18:37). If we're always in a hurry and surrounded by noise, we can't hear what God is saying. How could your family try to hear God's voice more?

↬ Why do you think God so rarely speaks in an audible voice to people?

## KA-BOOM!

Job compared God's voice to what sound? (Job 40:9)

# Praying the Bible Together

Dear Lord Jesus,

You have called each of us by name (John 10:3). And You have promised we'll recognize the sound of Your voice.

Your Word says: *I know my sheep and my sheep know me....
They...will listen to my voice* (John 10:14,16). When we don't recognize Your voice, please keep trying until we say, "Speak, for your servant is listening" (1 Sam. 3:10).

You tell us, *Be still, and know that I am God* (Ps. 46:10). When we get too busy to hear You, help us to slow down, get quiet, and really listen.

Thank You for Your promise: *Whether you turn to the right or to the left, your ears will hear a voice behind you, saying, "This is the way; walk in it"* (Isa. 30:21). When we get confused about what to do, help us to listen for Your direction.

Thank You that You speak to us through Your Word, through our parents and Christian friends, through what our hearts tell us, and through little events during the day. Open our spiritual ears to hear You.

Amen.

**TRUTH TO GO**
I will listen for the still, small voice.
(1 Kings 19:12)

# 21 | In a World of Hurt

*I saw the tears of the oppressed—and they have no comforter; power was on the side of their oppressors—and they have no comforter.... I have thought deeply about all that goes on here in the world, where people have the power of injuring each other.*

ECCLESIASTES 4:1, NIV; 8:9, TLB

*O Lord, how long will you look on?*

PSALM 35:17

Almost every day in the news, terrible things happen—robberies, rapes, murders, kids killing kids. Sometimes you wonder, *Where is God?*

But God doesn't promise a quick fix. Because humans sin, people will experience hurt and injustice. However, God has promised that He will always be with us. He has asked us to be His hands and feet on earth now, helping those in trouble (1 Cor. 3:9). And one day Jesus will return. He will bring justice. He will make everything fair and wipe away every tear (Matt. 5:19; Isa. 34:8; Rev. 21:4).

### FAMILY TALK

- Why do you think God doesn't just flick evil leaders off of the planet, fix the problems of the poor, and bring perfect justice to this world?
- Pray for people you know personally or people in the news today who have suffered because of crime or oppression.

### WISE GUY

Who wrote Ecclesiastes? (Hint: He was one of David's sons.)

# Praying the Bible Together

Dear God,

Thank You for understanding and welcoming our hard questions. Not only that, but You also invite us to look for answers (Prov. 25:2). Help us to do all we can to bring Your love to this hurting world. Remind us of what we *know* to be true about You from the Bible:

- You, O Lord, are love (1 John 4:16).
- You are just and fair (Deut. 32:4).
- You are good and patient (Nah. 1:7; 2 Pet. 3:9).
- You have the power to do anything (Jer. 32:17).
- You take care of us (Ps. 23).
- And one day, You will make everything right (Jer. 9:24).

Thank You that our family can count on You in a sometimes cruel and scary world. You hold our family in Your hands. We rest in Your care today.

Amen.

**TRUTH TO GO**
God is good, even in a bad world.
(Ps. 146:10)

# 22 | Dirty Feet

*Jesus...rose from supper and laid aside His garments, took a towel and girded Himself. After that He poured water into a basin and began to wash the disciples' feet, and to wipe them with the towel.*

JOHN 13:3-5, NKJV

Traveling in Bible times was a dirty business! Most people wore sandals; the roads and paths were dusty (and people walked everywhere), so travelers' feet were usually dirty. When a guest arrived, a host's wife or servant would wash the visitor's feet as a sign of welcome.

Jesus shocked His disciples one evening after dinner when He bent down to wash their feet. Think of it: the King of the universe cleaning other men's feet like any ordinary servant!

Jesus wanted to show His disciples how they should love and serve each other. He said, "Now that I, your Lord and Teacher, have washed your feet, you also should wash one another's feet." (John 13:14).

### FAMILY TALK

↬ Sometimes it's easy to think we're too good to do certain tasks—especially the messy or humbling ones. What are these tasks in your family? Who does them? How can they be shared more fairly?

↬ Think of some way you'd like to be served, then assign these "foot-washing" tasks to one another (set a time limit for the task and a completion time). When everyone is done, talk about how it felt to serve and be served.

### "NOT ME, LORD!"

Who didn't want Jesus to wash his feet? (John 13:6-9)

# Praying the Bible Together

Lord of All,

We confess that it's hard for us to humbly serve each other. But with Your help, we know we can! Help us to become expert "foot washers."

We pray with Your Word today:

> Whatever we do,
> help us to work at it with all our heart,
> as working for the Lord,
> not for men,
> since we know that we will receive
> an inheritance from the Lord as our reward.
> It is the Lord Christ we are serving (Col. 3:23-24)!
> We want to serve one another in love today (Gal. 5:13).
> You are our example, Lord Jesus.
> When You came to earth, You made yourself nothing—
> even though You were God—
> and You humbled Yourself
> and took the role and nature of a servant (Phil. 2:6-8).

Help us to be more and more like You every day. Because we love You and pray in Your name.

Amen.

**TRUTH TO GO**
Jesus was a humble servant.
(Phil. 2:7)

# 23 | Thanks a Lot!

*As he was going into a village, ten men who had leprosy met him. They stood at a distance and called out in a loud voice, "Jesus, Master, have pity on us!" When he saw them, he said, "Go, show yourselves to the priests." And as they went, they were cleansed. One of them, when he saw he was healed, came back, praising God in a loud voice. He threw himself at Jesus' feet and thanked him—and he was a Samaritan. Jesus asked, "Were not all ten cleansed? Where are the other nine? Was no one found to return and give praise to God except this foreigner?"*

LUKE 17:12-18

This story reminds us that it's easy to take God for granted. All ten men were healed of leprosy, a disease that left people disfigured and crippled. But only one came back to thank Jesus. The thankful man was a Samaritan, from a group of people who didn't like Jews. But he came back to thank Jesus "with a loud voice."

When God answers our prayers, we should give Him thanks and not just a quick, "Hey, I got what I wanted! Cool!" God deserves our heartfelt gratitude. Besides, we miss out on joy when we forget to praise Him.

### FAMILY TALK

↪ Have you ever given a nice present to someone or loaned something valuable to a friend who didn't thank you? How did it make you feel?

↪ List ten things you are most thankful for. Then think of a way to praise God "with a loud voice" for what He's done.

### AN AFFLICTED KING

What king suffered from leprosy? (2 Chron. 26)

# Praying Psalm 136 Together

Praiseworthy God,

Today, we give thanks to You, for You are good.

*His love endures forever* (vs. 1).

We give thanks to the God of gods.

*His love endures forever* (vs. 2).

We give thanks to the Lord of lords.

*His love endures forever* (vs. 3).

To Him who alone does great wonders.

*His love endures forever* (vs. 4).

To the One who remembered us in our low estate.

*His love endures forever* (vs. 23).

Who freed us from our enemies.

*His love endures forever* (vs. 24).

And who gives food to every creature.

*His love endures forever* (vs. 25).

We give thanks to the God of heaven.

*His love endures forever* (vs. 26)!

Amen.

**TRUTH TO GO**
Thank God!
(Ps. 136:1)

# 24 | "You'll Never Believe What I Heard!"

*A gossip betrays a confidence.... A gossip separates close friends.*

PROVERBS 11:13, 16:28

A gossip gives away someone else's secret. Or says unkind things about another person when they're not around. The Bible says we gossip because it feels kind of good, both to spread gossip and to hear it. "The words of a gossip are like choice morsels," says Proverbs 26:22. Why? Because when we hear about other people's problems, we feel better than they do. And when we spread gossip, we feel powerful because we know something that someone else doesn't. But gossiping is always sin because we hurt someone else just so we can feel better. And it hurts our relationships, too.

### FAMILY TALK

- What's the difference between gossiping and caring enough to share a concern about someone else? Can you come up with some rules for your family?
- If you tell a secret about Zach to Anna, will Anna trust you more or less with her own secrets?

### WORDS THAT HURT, WORDS THAT HEAL

The Bible says that when we talk about other people, our words can be like butter (Ps. 55:21), wind (Job 8:2), fire (James 3:6), a deep pit (Prov. 22:14), and apples of gold (Prov. 25:11). What could these words mean?

# Praying the Bible Together

Dear Lord,

Please forgive us for the times we've gossiped and hurt others by our words. Help us to remember to say kind things about others (Eph. 4:29)—or else to say nothing at all! Help us not to repeat bad news or criticism just because it makes us feel special.

We meditate on Your wisdom from the book of Proverbs today:

- Gossip separates close friends (16:28).
- Whoever spreads gossip is a fool (10:18).
- A gossip betrays a confidence, but a trustworthy person keeps a secret (11:13).
- The tongue that brings healing is a tree of life, but a deceitful tongue crushes the spirit (15:4).

Thank You, Lord, that You always speak well of us when Satan accuses us of being losers (Rev. 12:10). May we give gifts of kind words to others today—and keep gossip in the trash where it belongs.

In Your name we pray. Amen.

**TRUTH TO GO**
Gossip hurts everybody.
(Prov. 16:28)

# 25 | Bad Company

*Whoever spends time with wise people will become wise. But whoever makes friends with fools will suffer.*

PROVERBS 13:20, ICB

Have you ever heard someone say something like, "Oh that Nick guy—he's no good! Just look at the people he hangs out with!"

The Bible says, "Want to grow up to be a fool? Just hang out with fools." It's true! Your friends rub off on you. Lazy friends make you lazier. Angry friends make you angrier. Smart friends make you smarter. And so on.

Even if you manage not to let your friends rub off on you (which isn't likely), others will still misjudge you because they'll assume you are just the same as the kids you spend time with.

God wants us to be kind and helpful to everyone. But we should be best friends only with people we want to become more and more like!

### FAMILY TALK

- Where's the line between being an acquaintance and being a friend? Try to come up with practical guidelines to help your family choose good friends.
- Do you think watching and liking a TV character who is rude, immoral, or irresponsible is the same as spending time in bad company? Why or why not?

### GOOD BUDDIES

King David picked good friends. His best friend once saved his life. What was the friend's name? (1 Sam. 20)

# Praying Proverbs Together

Dear God,

The Bible is so clear on the dangers of wrong friends: "Do not envy wicked men, do not desire their company" (24:1); "Do not join those who drink too much wine" (23:20); "My son, if sinners entice you, do not give in to them" (1:10).

You know we want to choose good friends, but we need Your wisdom, Lord. Help us to know how to be fair judges of character. The Bible says a bad friend is someone who:

- loses his temper (12:16; 29:11)
- is reckless (14:16)
- ignores her parent's discipline (15:5)
- repeats his mistakes (26:11)
- spreads gossip (10:18)
- starts quarrels (20:3)

Thank You for this wisdom from Your Word. Thank You that good friends can make our whole life better and draw us closer to You. Amen.

**TRUTH TO GO**
The best friends help me be my best.
(Prov. 13:20)

# 26 | Shh…It's a Secret!

*When Delilah saw that [Samson] had told her everything, she sent word to the rulers of the Philistines, "Come back once more. He has told me everything." So the rulers of the Philistines returned with the silver in their hands. Having put him to sleep on her lap, she called a man to shave off the seven braids of his hair, and so began to subdue him. And his strength left him.*

JUDGES 16:18-19

*[Love] always protects.*

1 CORINTHIANS 13:7

Have you ever told someone a secret and then discovered that they'd blabbed it to the world? That's what happened to Samson, the strongest man in the Bible. Samson told his girlfriend, Delilah, the secret to his great strength—if his hair was cut off, he wouldn't have God's strength anymore. But the secret wasn't safe with Delilah because she didn't love him or his God. In exchange for money, she told the secret to Samson's enemies. While he was sleeping in her lap, they cut off Samson's hair and took him prisoner.

### FAMILY TALK

↪ Has someone ever betrayed your confidence? Have you betrayed someone else's? How did you feel? What happened?

↪ A friend keeps your secrets and protects you from your weaknesses. How can our family support each other instead of betray each other?

### HEAVY DUTY

What was the heaviest thing Samson ever lifted? (Judg. 16:3)

# Praying the Bible Together

Dear Lord,

Teach us to be loyal friends. When we know something about a brother or sister or friend that could hurt or embarrass them, help us to protect them. Save us from being Delilahs—friends who pretend to be loyal but aren't!

Give us the wisdom to know which friends we can trust and which we can't. Help us to stay away from trouble and companions who cause it. Help us to say as David did, "Away from me, you wrongdoers! I want to keep the commands of my God!" (from Ps. 119:115).

If we ever get trapped in a dangerous relationship, please protect us from evil (Ps. 121:7). Hide us in Your strength when we are weak or foolish (Ps. 31:20).

Teach us how to be the kind of friends who help others up when they fall (Eccles. 4:10).

In Your name we pray. Amen.

**TRUTH TO GO**
Love always protects.
(1 Cor. 13:7)

# 27 | "Take It from Me"

*Listen to advice and accept instruction.*

PROVERBS 19:20

*The way of a fool seems right to him, but a wise man listens to advice.*

PROVERBS 12:15

It's amazing what these four words can do: *Take it from me.* For many of us the second we hear that someone's about to give us advice, we resist. We might even stop listening! *Don't tell me what to do!* we think. *I don't need your help!*

But the Bible tells us that we're wise to listen to advice, especially when it comes from Mom or Dad. King Solomon, the wisest man who ever lived, once wrote, "Listen to your father, who gave you life, and do not despise your mother" (Prov. 23:22). To his own son he wrote, "My son, keep your father's commands and do not forsake your mother's teaching. Bind them upon your heart forever; fasten them around your neck. When you walk, they will guide you; when you sleep, they will watch over you; when you awake, they will speak to you" (6:20-22).

### FAMILY TALK

⤚ Should we take advice from just anyone? What should be the standard?

⤚ Proverbs 15:22 says that there is safety in a multitude of counselors. Name three people whose counsel and advice you trust.

### POP TO THE RESCUE

When Moses faced a problem leading Israel, he took advice from his father-in-law. What was this wise man's name? (Exod. 18:24,27)

# Praying the Bible Together

Dear Heavenly Father,
Help us to listen and learn
from our teachers, our elders, our parents,
and other wise people You put in our life.
When we're confused,
show us who to ask for advice
and help us to do what they say.
It's only pride and laziness
that keep us from taking good advice.
Please forgive us, Lord.
And today we remember the starting place
for getting smarter:
> "The fear of the LORD is the beginning of
> wisdom" (Prov. 9:10).
Thank You that You are the best counselor of all!
In Your name we pray. Amen.

**TRUTH TO GO**
God's advice is to take advice.
(Prov. 12:15)

# 28 | You Look Terrific!

*How beautiful you are my darling!... Like a lily among thorns...*

SONG OF SONGS 1:15; 2:2

*He has clothed me with garments of salvation and draped about me the robe of righteousness. I am like a bridegroom in his wedding suit or a bride with her jewels.*

ISAIAH 61:10, TLB

What do you think God sees when He looks at you?

Though some days you feel unattractive or even ugly, your loving Father sees the real you—a work of art, a lily among thorns. You see, every day God promises to forgive our sins, free us from our past, and clothe us in the beautiful robes of Jesus. That's better than looking like a movie star!

Next time you look in the mirror and frown at what you see, remember that the One who knows you best thinks you look terrific!

### FAMILY TALK

→ Name one thing about your physical features that you don't care for. Then ask God to show you how to make the most of this "beauty mark."

→ Do you know someone who probably doesn't feel too beautiful? Plan something to say or do soon to remind her that God thinks she's awesome!

### MISS PERSIA

Who entered a beauty contest to win the right to become Queen— and won? (Esther 2:1-18)

# Praying the Bible Together

Dear Loving God,
Thank You that on days when I feel ugly,
You say to me, *Oh, how beautiful you are!*
　　(Song of Songs 4:1).
Thank You that when I make a mistake
and fall into sin,
You look at me and see the goodness of Jesus,
and You say, *Oh, how beautiful you are!*
Thank You that when I feel really ordinary—
about as special as a brown paper bag,
about as smart as a slug who says, "Please pass the salt"—
You know the *real* me.
You know all the good things You have planned for me
because You love me.
You think I'm a one-of-a-kind miracle!
And You're the God of the universe.
Why should I doubt You?
That's why I can believe You when You say,
*Oh, how beautiful you are!*
I love You, Lord!
Amen.

**TRUTH TO GO**
God thinks I'm drop-dead gorgeous!
(Song of Songs 4:1)

# 29 | People Pleasers?

*Am I now trying to win the approval of men, or of God? Or am I trying to please men? If I were still trying to please men, I would not be a servant of Christ.*

The apostle Paul cared more about what God thought of him than what people did. But that's a hard thing to do, isn't it? After all, we all want to be liked and approved of. We all want to feel accepted and even popular.

But God knows that if we make decisions based on the approval of others, sooner or later we'll have to go against Him. That's because what God values and what's popular are often very different.

But here's the good news: If we try to please God first, we will automatically please the right people in the right way!

### FAMILY TALK

↜ Do you remember a time when you tried so hard to please or impress someone else, you ended up behaving like a fool or compromising an important value? Was it peer pressure or your pride that led you astray? What could you have done differently?

### A CROWD PLEASER

When Jesus was put on trial, the governor handed Him over to be crucified to please the crowd even though he knew Jesus was innocent. What was his name? (Luke 23:13-23)

# Praying the Bible Together

Heavenly Father,

Jesus said He came to earth to do Your will (John 6:38). He said, "I always do what pleases him" (John 8:28-29). Show our family how to make You happy today, Father.

We want to "live a life worthy of the Lord and…please him in every way: bearing fruit in every good work, growing in the knowledge of God" (Col. 1:10).

Help us to present our bodies as living sacrifices, holy and acceptable to You. Give us the determination and power of Your Spirit to not be conformed to others, but to be transformed by the renewing of our minds so that we can show what is good by Your standards (Rom. 12:1-2). Father, You created us for Your pleasure (Rev. 4:11, KJV). Thank You that You have promised that if we

- please You with our actions and
- please You with our faith and
- please You by treating You with our very highest respect

You *will* answer our prayers.

Our prayer today is to be God pleasers in all our thoughts, words, and actions.

We pray in Jesus' name. Amen.

**TRUTH TO GO**
How can I please God today?
(Gal. 1:10)

# 30 | Donkey Talk

*Then the LORD opened the donkey's mouth, and she said to Balaam, "What have I done to you to make you beat me these three times?"... The angel of the LORD asked [Balaam], "Why have you beaten your donkey these three times? I have come here to oppose you because your path is a reckless one before me. The donkey saw me and turned away from me these three times. If she had not turned away, I would certainly have killed you by now, but I would have spared her."*

NUMBERS 22:28,32-33

A talking donkey? You bet! Balaam was on his way to put a curse on God's people. But when an angel of the Lord appeared with a sword in the road, the donkey saw it and was afraid. Because the donkey wouldn't budge—and spoke up—Balaam was saved from doing something very foolish.

God cares enough about us to try to stop us when we're headed down the wrong path. He may or may not send a talking donkey, but watch and listen—God is always trying to get your attention!

**FAMILY TALK**

↪ Have you ever been on your way to making a big mistake when God seemed to send something or someone to stop you? What did you learn from that experience?

**DONKEY RIDE**
What famous person in the New Testament rode into Jerusalem on a donkey? (Matt. 21:1-5)

# Praying the Bible Together

Dear Lord,

We don't want to head in the wrong direction as Balaam did that day on the road. This is what we pray today:

> Help us to trust in the Lord with all our heart
> and lean not on our own understanding.
> May we acknowledge You in all our ways,
> so that You can make our paths straight. (Prov. 3:5-6)

Keep us, Lord, from becoming rebellious or stubborn or proud. We don't want to be fools who, through their rebellious ways, suffer because of their sins (Ps. 107:17).

So help us, Lord, to pay attention to Your directions. Help us to hear You when You say, "Turn back!"

Thank You that You promise to instruct us and teach us what is right (Isa. 28:26). Thank You that You are always with us, holding us in Your hand (Ps. 73:23). Thank You for this promise today:

*Whether you turn to the right or to the left, your ears will hear a voice behind you, saying, "This is the way; walk in it"* (Isa. 30:21).

Amen.

**TRUTH TO GO**
Listen, listen, listen for His voice!
(Isa. 30:21)

# 31 | A Sure Foundation

*Unless the LORD builds the house, its builders labor in vain.*

PSALM 127:1

*Therefore everyone who hears these words of mine and puts them into practice is like a wise man who built his house on the rock. The rain came down, the streams rose, and the winds blew and beat against that house; yet it did not fall, because it had its foundation on the rock.*

MATTHEW 7:24-25

Jesus said that if we listened to His teaching and then went out and put it into practice, we would be laying a firm foundation for our lives. Then when trials come and we're tempted to doubt God, we won't be swayed.

But listening to Jesus' teaching and knowing what to do aren't the same as doing it! Jesus says that if we listen to Him but don't do what He says, our plans will come crashing down when hard times hit.

### FAMILY TALK

- Do a family Building Inspection. Ask, When hard things happen or our family is under stress, do we pull together or fall apart? "Always pull together" means you're building on rock. Give yourself a 10. "Always fall apart" means you're building on sand. Give yourself a 1. How does your family rate?
- What are some specific ways you could pull together in the week ahead?

### JESUS AT WORK

What kind of occupation did Jesus have before He began His ministry? (Mark 6:3)

# Praying the Bible Together

Lord Jesus,

We want to be a family who not only hears You but does what You say. But we need Your help!

So we come to You, our Great Builder, placing our trust in the plans You have drawn for us. We know they are good. You want to give us hope and an exciting future (Jer. 29:11).

Help us to act on every direction You give us. Then we know our foundation is secure. Built on solid rock (Ps. 71:3). Immovable, unshakable (Ps. 46:1-2). When the winds of trouble howl, seeking to enter through cracks in the plaster, our hearts will be secure and we will have no fear (Ps. 112:8). Even on stormy days, peace will dwell within our walls (Ps. 122:7).

We ask that Your covering of grace will be the roof of our home (Rom. 6:14).

And Lord, we ask for lots of windows—the ability to see Your beauty and respond in praise (Ps. 148).

And an open door—the gift of hospitality to strangers as well as friends (Heb. 13:1-2).

May the walls of our house echo with shouts of praise to You, Lord, because what You build *lasts* (Heb. 3:4)!

Amen.

**TRUTH TO GO**
Build on the Solid Rock.
(Matt. 7:24-25)

# 32 | Encouragement Spoken Here!

*Do not use harmful words in talking. Use only helpful words, the kind that build up and provide what is needed, so that what you say will do good to those who hear you.*

EPHESIANS 4:29, TEV

*But encourage one another daily, as long as it is called Today, so that none of you may be hardened by sin's deceitfulness.*

HEBREWS 3:13

We all like to hear encouraging words when we're tired, frustrated, or feel like we're failing. But the Bible says we should keep encouraging each other *all the time*—not just when someone looks sad. When you say to someone, "You're doing great!" or "I see how hard you're trying," it's like pumping extra strength into his spirit. And it doesn't cost you a thing!

### FAMILY TALK

↪ On a small piece of paper, write "Encouragement, Please!" Then in a few words write one activity or area of your life where you could really use some extra encouragement this week. Then trade with someone else in the family...and start giving and receiving that extra boost of support and appreciation.

↪ Make a list of your top ten favorite kinds of encouraging phrases, like: "Way to go!" "You're good at that!" "Everything will be okay," "Don't quit!" Then be sure to use them this week!

### "CHEER UP, GUYS"
Who did Paul send to Ephesus to encourage the Christians?
(Eph. 6:21-22)

# Praying the Bible Together

Dear Lord,

Thank You that we can pray for our family today. Please help us to learn how to encourage one another more and more (1 Thess. 5:11).

Lord, it's so easy in a family to say things that tear another's spirit down. Teach all of us how to say only what's helpful, the kinds of things that build up a person's spirit, encourage him, and provide what is good to those who hear (Eph. 4:29).

Thank You, God, that You loved us and by Your grace gave us eternal encouragement. And You Yourself encourage our hearts and strengthen us in every good deed and word (2 Thess. 2:16-17).

Remind us to say things like: "Everything's going to be okay," "You've come further than you think," "I love you just the way you are," and "I believe in you." These words are so powerful, and You love to hear us talk like this and mean it.

May this be said of our family: "That [name] family—They are so encouraging and comforting. They're always gently urging each other to live a worthy life!" (1 Thess. 2:12).

Amen.

**TRUTH TO GO**
Everyone needs encouragement every day.
(Heb. 3:13)

# 33 | Wonderful Shepherd

*The LORD is my shepherd, I shall not be in want.*

*I am the good shepherd; I know my sheep and my sheep know me—just as the Father knows me and I know the Father—and I lay down my life for the sheep.*

JOHN 10:14

Today it might sound strange to compare yourself to a shepherd. But the people listening to Jesus were very familiar with what a shepherd did. It was his job to find pasture and water for his sheep. He had to protect them from bad weather and wild animals. If a sheep wandered away, he had to go find it.

God compares Himself to a shepherd because it's a job that requires so much constant attention and loving care. But Jesus said He wasn't just an ordinary shepherd. He said, "I lay down My life for the sheep."

**FAMILY TALK**

↪ Here are a few things you should know about sheep: They can't defend themselves against wild animals; if they run out of food, they aren't very good at finding new food; if one wanders away, usually others wander off with it; they know who their shepherd is by the sound of his voice. What do these traits tell you about why Jesus said, "I am the good shepherd"?

↪ How do you recognize your Shepherd Jesus' voice?

**GOD'S LAMB**

Who was called the Lamb of God? (John 1:29)

# Praying Psalm 23 Together

Dear Great Shepherd,

Yes, You are this family's Shepherd. Because of this, we know we'll never be without anything we truly need (v. 1).

Make us lie down today in green pastures of plenty. Lead us beside the still waters of contentment and peace (v. 2). When we're weary, restore our love for You. Help us take only paths of righteous living, for Your name's sake (v. 3).

When daily life weighs us down, or the fear of death somehow casts a shadow over our family—make Your loving presence known to each of us. By Your own hand carry this family along, comfort us, and nudge us toward maturity (v. 4).

When enemies of our faith or our family attack us, show Your great power, Lord. Come through for us, God. Display Your lavish affection for our family *right under their noses* (v. 5)!

Yes, Lord, may Your unfailing goodness and tender mercies surround this home and this family all the days of our lives, and may we find our true home in Your presence forever (v. 6).

Amen.

**TRUTH TO GO**
The Lord is my shepherd.
(Ps. 23:1)

# 34 | The Armor of God

*The weapons we fight with are not the weapons of the world. On the contrary, they have divine power to demolish strongholds.*

2 CORINTHIANS 10:4

*Finally, be strong in the Lord and in his mighty power. Put on the full armor of God so that you can take your stand against the devil's schemes.*

EPHESIANS 6:10-11

When you're being tempted to do something wrong, make sure you reach for the right kind of help. Paul told the Ephesian Christians to put on God's armor. Don't reach for a stick or a gun (or any ordinary weapon). Since temptation is a spiritual fight, try God's spiritual armor instead:

- the belt of truth (don't listen to Satan's lies)
- the breastplate of righteousness (Jesus' holiness covers you and helps you do the right thing)
- the shield of faith (you can trust God to be strong for you)
- the helmet of salvation (if you've asked Jesus to be your Lord, you're safe for eternity)
- the sword of the Spirit (the Bible can help you hear God and follow Him)

### FAMILY TALK

Talk about the armor of God, piece by piece. Remember, a piece of armor keeps you safe from harm. So ask, How can this piece of armor help our family win against temptation?

### DRESS UP

Satan masquerades as what? (2 Cor. 11:14)

# Praying Ephesians 6 Together

Lord,

Today we pray that You would equip each of us for spiritual battles.

Help our whole family to put on Your full armor so that when we face temptation or any enemy of You, we may be able to stand our ground and keep on standing (v. 13).

Show us how to buckle the belt of truth around our waist and how to fasten the breastplate of righteousness in place (v. 14).

Fit our feet with shoes that are quick to spread the news of the gospel of peace (v. 15). Give us strength to take up the shield of faith, with which we can stop all the flaming arrows of Satan (v. 16).

Give each of us the helmet of salvation so that we will be Your children forever. And show us how to use the powerful sword of the Spirit, which is Your inspired Word (v. 17).

Help our family to keep getting better at praying. Through prayer we can stay in touch with You, our Heavenly Commander.

Each day, help us to stay alert to temptation or any kind of spiritual attack (v. 18). But even more, help us never to forget that by Your power we can always be winners. Because You are King over all—even over Satan.

In Jesus' name. Amen.

**TRUTH TO GO**
Did I put my armor on today?
(Eph. 6:11)

# 35 | The Bread of Life

*Man shall not live on bread alone, but on every word that proceeds out of the mouth of God.*

MATTHEW 4:4, NASB

When you skip breakfast and then forget about lunch, you start to get tired. By afternoon you feel cranky and weak, not to mention starving. As soon as you can, you eat something.

It's the same way with our spirits. If we don't "eat" enough of God's Word, or if we don't listen to the Lord as we should, we end up feeling yucky and empty inside. That's because we're hungry for God.

In the same way you are careful to feed your stomach, be careful to feed your soul and "eat what is good!"

## FAMILY TALK

Estimate the average amount of time each day your family spends buying groceries, helping to prepare a meal, or eating food. Then add up how much time you are spending taking in "The Bread of Life" (reading your Bible and thinking about what it means for you). Is your spirit turning into skin and bones? If so, how can you change this?

## A HUNGRY CROWD

If Jesus is around, how many people can get full on five loaves of bread and two fish? (John 6:1-13)

# Praying the Bible Together

Lord,
Thank You that You are
"the living bread that came down from heaven"
    (John 6: 51).
You came down to us from heaven to give us life.
You said, "If anyone eats of this bread,
he will live forever" (6:51).
Today we want to fill our hearts
and quench our thirsty spirits
with Your living water (7:38).
We want the food You offer
because it never spoils (6:27).
Today may every snack and drink
and meal and dessert
remind us of how much we also need to feed our spirits.
Make us hungrier for You, God!
Help us to never forget
that we can't live on bread alone,
but that we also need to live on
every word You tell us (Matt. 4:4).
Amen.

**TRUTH TO GO**
I need to feed my spirit every day.
(Matt. 4:4)

# 36 | Dumb and Dumber

*Now a man named Ananias, together with his wife Sapphira, also sold a piece of property. With his wife's full knowledge he kept back part of the money for himself.... Peter said to [Sapphira], "How could you agree to test the Spirit of the Lord? Look! The feet of the men who buried your husband are at the door, and they will carry you out also."*

ACTS 5:1-2,9

Acts tells the story of the church in its first years. The Christians spent many hours each week meeting together to pray and worship. Many sold all their belongings and gave what they had to the church.

Then a couple named Ananias and Sapphira decided to cheat. They sold their property and kept part of the money. But that wasn't really the problem. They pretended that what they gave to the church was the full amount. Peter knew they were lying. On the same day, they both died.

The whole church learned three painful but powerful lessons that day: Don't lie to God, don't pretend to be more generous than you are, and don't love money more than God.

### FAMILY TALK

↪ Both Ananias and Sapphira knew they were in the wrong. Maybe they tried to tell themselves it was the other's fault. Have you ever blamed someone else for your own wrong choices? What should you do instead?

### THE BUCK STOPS HERE

During Joshua's campaign to conquer the Promised Land, a certain man and his family stole from the Lord and jeopardized everyone else's safety. He also died for his sin. Who was he? (Josh. 7)

# Praying the Bible Together

Dear Lord,

We do not ever want to be like Ananias and Sapphira! Save us from being dumb and dumber! Please forgive us for the times when we have tried to cheat or have tried to "pass the buck" for our own wrong behavior or have failed to stand up to someone who was doing the wrong thing.

Together may we honor You by keeping our commitments and by sharing with others what is ours. Help us to be loyal to You, even when we think we could get away with cheating.

Thank You for Your promise that

> Only those with clean hands and pure hearts...
> will receive a blessing from the Lord. (Ps. 24:4-5, ICB)

Amen.

**TRUTH TO GO**
It's dumb to try to cheat God.
(from Acts 5:9)

# 37 | The Right Thing to Do

*Children, the right thing for you to do is to obey your parents as those whom the Lord has set over you. The first commandment to contain a promise was: Honour thy father and thy mother that it may be well with thee, and that thou mayest live long on the earth.*

EPHESIANS 6:1-3, PHILLIPS

We all know that we're supposed to mind our parents and do what they say. But the Bible teaches this not just because they're our parents or because they're always right (of course, they're not!). It is because God wants things to turn out well for *us!* When we honor our parents, we line up our actions and attitudes with God's will in a way that allows Him to bless us.

God doesn't ask us to honor our parents only when we are young either. We should esteem and respect our parents even when we become parents ourselves.

### FAMILY TALK

- What do you think God means by the word "honor"? How does your family handle situations where kids and parents disagree? How is it possible to disagree with a parent and still honor him/her?
- God has advice for parents who want to be honored: "Fathers, don't over-correct your children, or you will take all the heart out of them" (Col. 3:21, Phillips). What do you think this means?

### WICKED SONS

What Old Testament priest had sons who didn't honor their father and came to a bad end as a result? (1 Sam. 2:22-25)

# Praying the Bible Together

Heavenly Father,

Thank You for the joy of families. Help each of us to carry out our role so that all Your promises come to pass in our lives. We pray today for a home environment of loving respect, where children practice good manners, consideration, obedience, and patience.

You have put parents, along with teachers and other leaders, in authority for a reason (Rom. 13:1). And You ask children to obey for a reason—so their lives will go better. Even Jesus lived under Your authority while on earth, saying that pleasing You and finishing the work You asked Him to do was like food to Him (John 4:34).

We pray that You would show us, as parents, how to have the kind of firm and yet loving hand that encourages sincere obedience from our children. Especially help our children choose obedience to us because they want to obey You. As they make a habit of respecting those in authority, thank You that You'll bless them in everything they do (Luke 19:17).

In Your name we pray. Amen.

**TRUTH TO GO**
I honor God when I honor my parents.
(Eph. 6:1-3)

# 38 | Second Chances

*When God saw what [the people of Nineveh] did and how they turned from their evil ways, he had compassion and did not bring upon them the destruction he had threatened.*

JONAH 3:10

Do you know the amazing story of Jonah? God told Jonah to go to the city of Nineveh to warn them about their evil ways. But Jonah didn't obey. Instead he got on a ship to sail across the sea. So God sent a great storm, and the ship began to sink. Jonah told the sailors it was all his fault and that if they threw him overboard the storm would stop.

So they did. *Splash!*

But before he could drown, God sent a huge fish to swallow Jonah. For three days and three nights he prayed inside the fish's belly. When the fish threw up Jonah onto dry land, God gave Jonah a second chance. This time, Jonah went to Nineveh and told them God would destroy their city if things didn't change. The people there were sorry, and God decided to have mercy on them and give them a second chance, just as He had done for Jonah.

## FAMILY TALK

Most of the time we don't *deserve* a second chance, but we sure *need* one. Do you need another chance to do the right thing in some responsibility or behavior today? Does another family member need a second chance *from you?*

## FISH FACE

When Jonah fled from the Lord and boarded that ship, what city was he headed to instead of Nineveh? (Jon. 1:3)

# Praying the Bible Together

God of Second Chances,

When we have chosen to go our own way, rather
than obey You, O Lord…

*Hear our cry for mercy* (from Ps. 28:2).

When waves engulf us, and deep waters surround us,
O Lord…

*Hear our cry for mercy.*

When, like Jonah, we are swallowed whole by the
trouble our sin has caused, O Lord…

*Hear our cry for mercy.*

Just as You forgave Jonah for his stubbornness and
rebellion,

we're sorry, and we ask, O Lord…

*Hear our cry for mercy.*

Thank You, Lord of Second Chances, that if we
confess our sins,

You are faithful and just and will forgive us (1 John 1:9).

Thank You, O Lord, that You…

*Hear our cry for mercy.*

In Your name we pray. Amen.

**TRUTH TO GO**
God gives second chances.
(Jon. 3:10)

# 39 | Veggies with Love

*Better a meal of vegetables where there is love than a fattened calf with hatred.*

PROVERBS 15:17

Maybe a fattened calf doesn't sound that tasty to you, but in Bible times it was the ultimate feast. Today you might say, "Better liver and onions (or something else you don't like) at a happy dinner table, than pizza and ice cream when everyone's fighting."

Even the most delicious dinner doesn't taste good if it is spoiled by arguments and tension. God is saying that love and harmony matter more in a family than what's on the menu.

## FAMILY TALK

- What are some ways your family can make mealtimes more pleasant and peaceful?
- How can your family show more gratitude to the one who cooks?

## INVISIBLE FOOD

Once when Jesus' disciples urged Him to eat, He told them, "I have food to eat that you know nothing about." What was it?
(John 4:31-34)

# Praying the Bible Together

Gracious Lord,
Your Word teaches that
veggies with love is a feast.
Help us to make harmony and smiles
and patience and forgiveness
and good listening and good humor
the most important food we serve
at our table!
Please help us to be grateful
for whatever food we are served—
and to make getting along
as important as getting full!
We don't want
a delicious meal with hatred.
We want to enjoy what You provide
with love.

Thank You, Father,
That even on macaroni-and-cheese weeks,
we are very, very blessed by You!
Amen.

**TRUTH TO GO**
Food tastes best with love.
(Prov. 15:17)

# 40 | The Right Place at the Right Time

*When Esther's words were reported to Mordecai, he sent back this answer:
"Do not think that because you are in the king's house you alone of all the
Jews will escape. For if you remain silent at this time, relief and deliverance
for the Jews will arise from another place.... Who knows but that you have
come to royal position for such a time as this?"*

ESTHER 4:12-14

King Xerxes had chosen young Esther as his next queen because she
was gorgeous—"lovely in form and features" (Esther 2:7). But God
probably chose her because she had nerves of steel. When her cousin
Mordecai found out about an evil plot to kill the Jews, he asked Esther
to risk her life by going to the king to plead for her people. (It was
against the law for people to talk to the king unless they'd first been
invited by him.) But when King Xerxes saw Esther, he was glad. When
he heard about the plan to kill her people, he stopped it immediately.

God puts all of us in certain places at certain times for special reasons. It's up to us to be courageous and available to Him.

### FAMILY TALK

- Talk about some other people in history who were in the right
  place at the right time.
- Think about the people you can influence and your special
  talents. Whom can you reach that others can't? Ask God to
  show you ways you can be part of His plans in your world.

### ROYAL JUSTICE
Who was the evil character plotting to kill the Jewish people?
What happened to him? (Esther 3:5-6; 7:10)

# Praying the Bible Together

Dear God,
Like Esther,
we want to be courageous,
available, and willing
for You to work through us.
You saw in a lovely orphan girl
someone who could stop
an evil plot against Your people.
What do You see in us
that we might have overlooked?
What talents or interests
do You want us to put to work for You today?
Help us to live carefully
and to make the most of every opportunity
    (Eph. 5:15-16).
We know You've brought us to this place,
to these people and these challenges,
for such a time as this.
Amen.

**TRUTH TO GO**
Make the most of every opportunity for God.
(Eph. 5:16)

# 41 | Time for Church

*Year after year this man [Elkanah] went up from his town to worship and
sacrifice to the LORD Almighty at Shiloh.*

1 SAMUEL 1:3

*Let us not give up meeting together, as some are in the habit of doing, but let
us encourage one another—and all the more as you see the Day approaching.*

HEBREWS 10:25

If you were going to make a list of Bible heroes, Elkanah probably
wouldn't get nominated. Most people don't even remember who he
was. Elkanah took his family to worship God regularly. He wasn't just
following the crowd either—most people in this time of Israel's history
weren't obeying God (Judg. 17:6). And Elkanah didn't just go to worship when things were going well—year after year, he and his wife
Hannah asked for a baby, but God hadn't given them one yet.

Today families are busier than ever. It takes a lot of effort to get the
whole family to church. But God says church is important for Christians—even if we're tired or don't feel like going. We need to worship
God, to learn more about Him, and be encouraged by other believers.

### FAMILY TALK

Talk about how each of you feels about church. Is there anything you could do to make going to church more meaningful
and enjoyable?

### A FAMOUS SON

Name the son God eventually gave to Elkanah and Hannah.
(1 Sam. 1:20)

# Praying the Bible Together

Dear Lord,

Today we thank You for our church family. We are so grateful that You bring other believers alongside us to teach and encourage us. Thank You that if we walk in the light, as You are in the light, we have fellowship one with another, and the blood of Jesus Christ cleanses us from all sin (1 John 1:7).

Give our family a fierce passion to be an active part of our church community. As we gather at church, help us to express love to each other. And help us to express love to You in psalms, hymns, and spiritual songs, making beautiful music in our hearts to You, Lord (Eph. 5:2,19)!

As we listen to our pastor and our Bible teachers, may Your words dwell in us richly, bringing us wisdom and making us more like You (Col. 3:16).

We want to be like the early church who spent a lot of time together, eating, praying, giving, and praising (Acts 2:42,45-47). As we meet, You've promised to knit our hearts together in love and give us a full assurance of Your amazing work in our lives (Col. 2:2, NASB).

We're Your family, Lord! Fill our hearts with joy next time we hear someone say, "Let us go to the house of the LORD" (Ps. 122:1).

Amen.

**TRUTH TO GO**
It is good to go to church.
(Heb. 10:25)

# 42 | "God Bless You!"

*The LORD bless you and keep you; the LORD make his face shine upon you and be gracious to you; the LORD turn his face toward you and give you peace.*

NUMBERS 6:24-26

These days when we hear someone say, "God bless you!" it usually means someone sneezed. That's because people used to think if you sneezed you were getting sick, and only God's blessing could prevent it.

But what does the word "blessing" mean in the Bible? It means to ask for God's special favor. When we give someone a blessing, it's a way of praying for them—right in front of them.

This blessing in Numbers was the priestly blessing that Aaron and his sons gave to the Israelites. A father was expected to give a special blessing to his firstborn son (Gen. 27). Paul often pronounced blessings in his letters to the Church (Rom. 15:13).

Today we can still ask God to bless others, based on His promises. For example, we might say to someone, "May God's peace that passes understanding be in your heart today!" (from Phil. 4:7).

### FAMILY TALK

↢ What kind of blessing do you need this week?

↢ Take a few minutes to list some blessings you could give to other family members, based on Scripture. (Hint: Put some of the blessings on the next page into your own words.) Then look for an opportunity to bless someone this week!

### RIVAL SIBLINGS

Which Old Testament twin brothers had a bitter fight over their father Isaac's blessing? (Gen. 27)

# Praying the Bible Together

*A Blessing for Encouragement:*
"May our Lord Jesus Christ himself and God our Father, who loved us and by his grace gave us eternal encouragement and good hope, encourage your hearts and strengthen you in every good deed and word" (2 Thess. 2:16-17).

*A Blessing for Spiritual Growth:*
"We have confidence in the Lord that you are doing and will continue to do the things we command. May the Lord direct your hearts into God's love and Christ's perseverance" (2 Thess. 3:4-5).

*A Blessing for Hope:*
"May the God of hope fill you with all joy and peace as you trust in him, so that you may overflow with hope by the power of the Holy Spirit" (Rom. 15:13).

**TRUTH TO GO**
God Bless You!
(Num. 6:24)

# 43 | "You're Good at That!"

*There are different kinds of gifts, but the same Spirit. There are different kinds of service, but the same Lord. There are different kinds of working, but the same God works all of them in all men.*

King David was good at writing psalms and playing the harp, among other things. Paul was good at preaching and teaching. Solomon was wise. What are you good at? Maybe it's a sport or an art form. Maybe you are really good at listening to people.

God has given each of us special talents. But Paul reminded the church in Corinth that no one is better than anyone else in God's eyes just because they have a certain gift. God needs all kinds of people for all kinds of jobs. He didn't give us talents so we can become proud or show off. He wants us to use our gifts to serve others (1 Pet. 4:10).

## FAMILY TALK

↝ Name three things you think you might be good at. If you can't decide, ask yourself, What do I enjoy doing? Or ask other family members what they think you do well.

↝ Decide on a new way that you can use one of these talents for God, and make a plan to put it in action.

## MISUSED TALENT

The daughter of Herodias used a special talent to impress King Herod. What was it? (Matt. 14:6-12)

# Praying the Bible Together

Lord,

Thank You for making each of us unique and giving us different interests, passions, and talents. Truly, You are the giver of every good gift (James 1:17)!

We thank You for giving us special interests and abilities, from basketball to ballet, from team roping to playing the tuba. But we ask also for spiritual gifts we can use to build up other believers—gifts like teaching, service, comforting others, and healing (1 Cor. 12:8-10).

Today we pray that each of us would want and value the treasures You have invested in us—for our own benefit and for the blessing of others (1 Cor. 14:1). And beyond that, fill us with a lifelong desire to use any talent—be it physical, mental, or spiritual—to serve You (1 Cor. 12:4-11).

Help each of us in this family to encourage each other to persist in our areas of talent. May we be like Paul who urged Timothy not to neglect the gift God had given him (1 Tim. 4:14). Help us to work hard to make the most of the gifts You've given us—to practice, learn, and train with patience.

Thank You for Your promise, Lord, that whatever good work You begin in us, You will help us take it as far as we can (Phil. 1:6).

In Your name. Amen.

**TRUTH TO GO**

I should use my talents to serve others.

(1 Pet. 4:10)

# 44 | When Bad Guys Go Good

*At once he [Saul] began to preach in the synagogues that Jesus is the Son of God. All those who heard him were astonished and asked, "Isn't he the man who raised havoc in Jerusalem among those who call on this name? And hasn't he come here to take them as prisoners to the chief priests?" Yet Saul grew more and more powerful and baffled the Jews living in Damascus by proving that Jesus is the Christ.*

ACTS 9:20-22

No wonder the people in Damascus were confused. This man, Saul, was supposed to be the number-one enemy of the Christians. He had been putting Christians in jail—and now he was preaching about Christ?

But Saul's conversion was real. He had in fact received Christ and been baptized. Saul went on to be renamed Paul, and he became a great apostle and evangelist. You see, no one is ever too evil or too hopeless for Christ to save him and use him for good!

## FAMILY TALK

⟶ Name someone you know, or someone you know about, who you think would never receive Christ in a million years.

⟶ Come up with a plan to witness to and pray for this person. Maybe you could write him/her a letter or, if you know this person, invite him/her to a church or youth group.

## "BUT NOW I SEE"

When Jesus first confronted Saul, what happened to Saul's eyes? (Acts 9:1-19)

# Praying the Bible Together

Jesus,

Today we are filled with gratefulness for Your love! We are among those sinners who, like Saul, desperately needed saving, Lord. And You saved us! That's why we want to remember that there is no person You don't want to save (2 Pet. 3:9)—even the most sinful among us.

We thank You that our righteousness comes not from anything good we do, but only from faith in You, Jesus. All of us have sinned and lost our way. We know so well that no one is good apart from You. And the only reason any of us in this family is saved is because of Your grace (Rom. 3:22-24).

Thank You that You came into this world to save sinners like Saul. Even though he was a blasphemer, a persecutor, and a violent man, You showed him mercy! And in doing so, You prove to us how great your mercy really is (1 Tim. 1:13,15-16).

Today, we rejoice in Your great mercy, Jesus. And we say with Paul, "The grace of our Lord was poured out on me abundantly, along with the faith and love that are in Christ Jesus" (1 Tim. 1:14).

Amen.

**TRUTH TO GO**

There is no sinner that God doesn't want to save.

(2 Pet. 3:9)

# 45 | "I Promise!"

*He has given us his very great and precious promises.*

2 PETER 1:4

Has someone ever promised to do something for you—but never did it? It's good to know that when God makes a promise, He will keep it. Not just usually. Not just most of the time. But always!

The Bible is full of promises from God that He wants us to count on. They are like gifts that He has given us. All we have to do is to take off the wrapping and say, "Thank You, Lord! I receive this promise!"

## FAMILY TALK

- Can you name your favorite promise from God? Why does this mean so much to you?
- How are God's promises different from the kinds of promises some people make?

## COLOR MY WORLD

When God made a promise to Noah that He would never flood the world again, what did He give as a reminder of His promise? (Gen. 9:16)

# Praying the Bible Together

Dear Heavenly Father,

We thank You for Your priceless promises. How great it is to know for sure that You are a God of Your word (Num. 23:19). Today we want to remember and claim these "great and precious promises" for our family:

- *Never will I leave you; never will I forsake you* (Heb. 13:5).
- *I am your provider and protector, comforter, and friend* (from Ps. 23:1; 27:1; Isa. 25:8; John 15:15).
- *If two of you on earth agree about anything you ask for, it will be done for you* (Matt. 18:19).
- *Everyone who receives me and believes in my name becomes a child of God* (from John 1:12).
- *My kindness, mercies, and love for you are inexhaustible!* (from Ps. 18:50; Lam. 3:22; Jer. 31:3).

It's with deeply felt thanks, Lord, that we claim Your loving promises for this family. Let each promise be a bright, colorful rainbow of encouragement in our lives today. "For he who promised is faithful!" (Heb. 10:23).

Amen.

**TRUTH TO GO**
God keeps His promises.
(Heb. 10:23)

# 46 | Born Again

*Now there was a man of the Pharisees named Nicodemus, a member of the Jewish ruling council. He came to Jesus at night and said, "Rabbi, we know you are a teacher who has come from God. For no one could perform the miraculous signs you are doing if God were not with him." In reply Jesus declared, "I tell you the truth, no one can see the kingdom of God unless he is born again." "How can a man be born when he is old?" Nicodemus asked.*

JOHN 3:1-4

Poor Nicodemus. He couldn't understand what Jesus was saying. "Surely he cannot enter a second time into his mother's womb to be born!" he exclaimed (John 3:4). What Jesus meant is that it's not enough for a person to just be religious or go to church. When we receive Christ, we become whole new people from the inside out. Paul told new Christians, "If anyone is in Christ, he is a new creation; the old has gone, the new has come!" (2 Cor. 5:17).

### FAMILY TALK

- We become born again as soon as we ask Jesus to be our Savior and forgive us of our sins. Do you have a special memory of the moment when you were "born again?" (If anyone in the family has doubts about their salvation, offer to pray with them.)

- Some people say that they came to faith in Christ over time. Do you think it matters either way?

### HELPING OUT

Jesus must have made an impact on Nicodemus because he helped to bury Jesus after the crucifixion. Who was the rich man who provided the tomb? (John 19:38-41)

# Praying the Bible Together

Dear Lord Jesus,
We are so thankful that You cared enough
to answer questions from people like Nicodemus
who wanted to know the truth.
We pray today for the ones we know
who need so desperately to know You.
We pray especially for _____, _____, and _____.
Thank You for placing these people in our lives.
We pray with Paul that whenever we open our mouths,
words may be given us
so that we will fearlessly make known
the good news of the gospel (Eph. 6:19).
Thank You for loving this world, God,
so much that You sent your Son to die
so we might be born again
and live forever (John 3:16).
We thank and praise You for this today.
Amen.

**TRUTH TO GO**
We must be born again!
(John 3:3)

# 47 | Somebody Important

*For we know…that he has chosen you.*

1 THESSALONIANS 1:4

You feel great when you're chosen to play on a team—and *terrible* when you're left standing on the sidelines! Everyone else is having fun, but you feel unwanted and rejected.

Well, here's some good news: Jesus chose you! In His eyes, no matter how many others He loves, He has picked you out. One time Jesus told a story about this. He said even if a shepherd knows where ninety-nine out his one hundred sheep are, he will leave the flock to look for the one lamb that has strayed. Jesus was saying He came to the world to find each of us—one at a time!

Jesus has chosen you to be on His team. And here's the best news: He really likes you too!

### FAMILY TALK

- Name two things about yourself that make you special. (Hint: a talent, a favorite activity, a special relationship, something about how you look, or something you've accomplished in the past.) Do you need the family to help you see them? Thank God for these gifts.

- Do you know someone who probably doesn't feel special? How could you communicate to that person that he or she is indeed someone important—especially in God's eyes?

### CHOSEN ONES

The words "God's chosen people" are used to describe two groups of people in the Bible. Who are they? (Isa. 44:1; 1 Pet. 2:9)

# Praying the Bible Together

Dear Heavenly Father,
Thank You that You know me well (Ps. 139:1).
    I am made in Your image (Gen. 1:26-27)!
That means something about me reminds me of You!
If I believe in You, I can take Your family name—
    "Christian" (John 1:12).
You made just one of me, and when You did, You
    were already thinking of good things I would do.
You call me "your workmanship" like a proud artist
    (Eph. 2:10).
You call me "holy and dearly loved" (Col. 3:12) like a
    loving Father.
You came from heaven to make me great (Ps. 18:35)
    and die for me (John 3:16).
Your Spirit lives in my heart (1 Cor. 3:16),
    and one day, You'll give me a crown that will last
        forever (1 Cor. 9:25).
That's why I feel special today.
Thank You, Heavenly Father!
Amen.

**TRUTH TO GO**
I'm always on God's mind.
(Ps. 139)

# 48 | Lying Lion

*Your enemy, the devil, prowls around like a roaring lion looking for someone to devour.*

1 PETER 5:8

*Submit yourselves, then, to God. Resist the devil, and he will flee from you.*

JAMES 4:7

The Bible paints a pretty scary picture of the devil. Imagine a huge hungry lion who is out hunting for his next meal—and he spots you! Yikes!

Isn't it good to know that God promises you can escape? When you are tempted to do something wrong, you can say no. Tell the devil flat out, "I choose to obey God! Go away!" And watch him run.

## FAMILY TALK

- Why do you think we so often forget about the devil's role when we are tempted?
- Share a time when you were tempted but you resisted—and won. How did you feel?

## DESERT TEMPTATIONS

How many times did Satan tempt Jesus when He was praying and going without food in the desert? (Luke 4:1-13)

# Praying the Bible Together

Heavenly Father,

Save us from evil! Don't let temptations trap any member of this family. Thank You for promising us that:

*If we will resist the devil, he will run* (from James 4:7).

When little sins begin to look as good to us as cotton candy, help us to remember that:

*If we resist the devil, he will run.*

Thank You, Father, that when the devil sees You inside of us, he becomes like the cowardly lion in *The Wizard of Oz*. We are so glad that:

*If we resist the devil, he will run!*

What a relief! We choose today to submit our whole hearts to You, God. And we thank You for being so much greater and stronger than that lying lion, Satan.

In Jesus' name we pray. Amen.

**TRUTH TO GO**
If I resist the devil, he will run!
(James 4:7)

# 49 | "Help, I'm Sinking!"

*During the fourth watch of the night Jesus went out to them, walking on the lake. When the disciples saw him walking on the lake, they were terrified. "It's a ghost," they said, and cried out in fear. But Jesus immediately said to them: "Take courage! It is I. Don't be afraid." "Lord, if it's you," Peter replied, "tell me to come to you on the water." "Come," he said. Then Peter got down out of the boat, walked on the water and came toward Jesus. But when he saw the wind, he was afraid and, beginning to sink, cried out, "Lord, save me!" Immediately Jesus reached out his hand and caught him. "You of little faith," he said, "why did you doubt?"*

MATTHEW 14:25-31

Howling wind. Dark night. Crashing waves. Scared sailors. Must be an adventure story, right? Then the frightened sailors see someone—or maybe it's something—walking on the water. Uh-oh! Must be a ghost story. And now they're *really* scared!…

But Jesus' first words to them are, "Take courage. It is I. Don't be afraid."

### FAMILY TALK

- The Bible says to "fix our eyes on Jesus, the author and perfecter of our faith" (Heb. 12:2). How can you keep your eyes on Jesus so you don't get afraid?
- Is there anything you're afraid of today? How can Jesus help you?

### GLUB, GLUB

Who's another famous sinking sailor in the Bible? (book of Jonah)

# Praying the Bible Together

Dear Lord Jesus,
Thank You that You are a strong God.
You have power over the wind and the water
and any problem we might face today.
Thank You for this story about Peter.
You didn't let him sink,
and when we get in trouble,
You will rescue us, too.
We don't have to be afraid.
Peter proved You were right, Jesus, when You said,
"Apart from me you can do nothing" (John 15:5).

If any storms come up today
help us keep our eyes on You because Your Word says:
"I can do everything through him
who gives me strength" (Phil. 4:13).

Thank You. In Jesus' name. Amen.

**TRUTH TO GO**
I will keep my eyes on Jesus.
(Heb. 12:2)

# 50 | Friends to the End

*Love each other as I have loved you. Greater love has no one than this, that he lay down his life for his friends.... I have called you friends.*

JOHN 15:13,15

Do you remember people who said they were your friends then did something to prove they weren't? Maybe they spread a rumor about you. Or didn't want to spend time with you. Maybe they were your friends only when someone they liked better wasn't around.

Real friends are loyal. That means they stand by you when it's easy *and* when it's hard. "A friend loves at all times" (Prov. 17:17). According to Jesus, the highest test of friendship is if one friend is willing to die for the other.

One of the nicest things Jesus called the disciples was "friends." And He proved He meant it. He took care of them, prayed for them, spent time with them, and shared His thoughts and feelings with them. He didn't stop being a friend when they let him down.

He even died for them!

### FAMILY TALK

- Do you feel a special bond with one of your friends? How could you let that person know?
- Name three things that you appreciate most about one of your best friends. What do you think your friend would say about you?

### FALSE FRIEND

Jesus was betrayed by a "friend." Who? (Matt. 10:4)

# Praying the Bible Together

Dear Lord and Friend,

Today we pray that You will bless us with many friends—especially good friends who can help us become the people you want us to be. May our closest friends be ones who love You and do what it is right (Prov. 13:20).

Bring us friends who are as loyal as a brother or sister (Prov. 18:24). Help us to choose friends who will be there to help us get back on our feet when we fall (Eccles. 4:10). And help our family to want to be that kind of friend, too. We want to be trusted friends at all times.

Show us when we should lay down our rights or put aside what we want to help out a friend in need. Because "greater love has no one than this, that he lay down his life for his friends" (John 15:13).

Thank You for calling Your disciples Your friends. Thank You for being our very best friend for life! We want to be Your friend, too, today by loving You enough to do exactly what You ask us to do (v. 14).

We pray in Your name. Amen.

**TRUTH TO GO**
A friend loves at all times.
(Prov. 17:17)

# 51 | Testing, Testing...

*Now faith is being sure of what we hope for and certain of what we do not
see.... By faith Abraham, when God tested him, offered Isaac as a sacrifice.
He who had received the promises was about to sacrifice his one and only
son, even though God had said to him, "It is through Isaac that your off-
spring will be reckoned."*

HEBREWS 11:1,17-18

It was one hard test after another. God asked Abraham to leave home
and go on a journey (but God wouldn't say where). Then God told
Abraham he would have millions of descendants (but his wife, Sarah,
couldn't get pregnant). Then after God finally did give them a son,
God gave Abraham his final exam: "Take your son, your only son,
Isaac, whom you love," God said, "and...sacrifice him...as a burnt
offering" (Gen. 22:2).

Kill his son to show his faith? Yikes! But Abraham said, "Okay,
God. I trust You enough." Luckily for Isaac, it turned out to be only a
test. When God saw Abraham's radical faith, He stopped the sacrifice.

## FAMILY TALK

- According to Hebrews 11:1, what is faith?
- What other Bible story does Abraham sacrificing his son
  remind you of?
- Has God asked your family to do any hard things to test your
  faith?

## ONLY BY FAITH

In Hebrews 11:8-12, find three things Abraham did by faith.

# Praying Hebrews 11 Together

Gracious Lord,

Today I ask that You will help our family to be certain about Your love and Your presence, even when we can't see or touch those realities (v. 1). You who made the universe out of nothing (v. 3), even when we can't see You, we know You're at work. May each member of our family develop the kind of faith that is pleasing and acceptable to You (v. 4).

Teach us, Lord, how to be a hero of faith today:

Like Enoch, who walked with You, may we also walk closely with You. Thank You that if we seek You earnestly, You will reward us (vv. 5-6).

By faith, let us be like Noah. He obeyed You and took years to build the biggest boat anyone had ever seen—and it hadn't even rained a drop yet! Help us believe whatever You say, no matter what others think (v. 7).

By faith, we want to be like Abraham who followed You wherever You led and did whatever You said (vv. 8-10).

Since trust in You is so important to You, Lord, please help us to grow strong in it. We want to be heroes of faith in Your eyes.

Amen.

**TRUTH TO GO**
Faith pleases God.
(Heb. 11:6)

# 52 | The Lord's Prayer

*This, then, is how you should pray: "Our Father in heaven, hallowed be your name, Your kingdom come, your will be done on earth as it is in heaven. Give us today our daily bread. Forgive us our debts, as we also have forgiven our debtors. And lead us not into temptation, but deliver us from the evil one."*

MATTHEW 6:9-13

You've probably heard this prayer before—maybe at church. Jesus spoke this prayer after His disciples requested, "Teach us to pray" (Luke 11:1). That's why it has become the best example for how we can talk to God.

The first three parts of the prayer talk about who God is. The last three parts talk about our needs—food for the body, forgiveness for our wrongs, and help with temptations we face. Jesus prayed often because He, too, wanted to talk to His Father. That's why His prayer begins, "Our Father in heaven."

### FAMILY TALK

➥ Why do you think Jesus needed to pray—even though He Himself was God?

➥ If anyone in the family doesn't have The Lord's Prayer memorized, learn part of it each day until you all know it by heart.

### HUNGRY?

If we ask our Father for food, what WON'T He give us?
(Luke 11:11-12)

# Praying Matthew 6 Together

*Our Father in Heaven,*
> Thank You that Jesus showed us and taught us
> how to talk to You.

*Hallowed be Your name.*
> We come before You with respect and love today.

*Your kingdom come, Your will be done,*
> May we live as You want us to live—

*on earth as...in heaven,*
> especially in this home and in our family.

*Give us today our daily bread.*
> Because without Your taking care of us, we'd starve.

*Forgive us our debts, as we also have forgiven our debtors.*
> Wash away our sins, and help us to forgive others.

*And lead us not into temptation, but deliver us from the
evil one.*
> Save us from our own wrong desires and all
> Satan's tricks.

*For Yours is the kingdom and the power and the glory
forever.*
> Because You are Lord of our family.
> Amen.

**TRUTH TO GO**
Prayer is talking to my Heavenly Father.
(Matt. 6:9)

119

# 53 | Just Like Stars

*Do everything without complaining or arguing, so that you may become blameless and pure, children of God without fault in a crooked and depraved generation, in which you shine like stars in the universe as you hold out the word of life.*

PHILIPPIANS 2:14-16

*Those who are wise will shine like the brightness of the heavens, and those who lead many to righteousness, like the stars for ever and ever.*

DANIEL 12:3

God wants to make us stars! Not the Hollywood kind of star who wins Academy Awards, fame, and fortune—but the kind who brightens the world with His light. He wants our whole family to be glowing proof of God's love, just like stars sparkling in the night sky.

### FAMILY TALK

- Name someone you know who you think shines like a bright star for God. What makes that person different?
- Go outside tonight and look up at the sky. Do you see the stars? They are millions of miles away, but we can still see them. Talk about specific ways you can shine so others will see Jesus in you.

### THE BRIGHTEST STAR

Jesus is sometimes called the Morning Star (Rev. 22:16), which we now know is really a planet. Which planet?

# Praying the Bible Together

Blessed Morning Star,
Help our family to shine out in this world because we treat each other well.

For You have told us, *Now you are light in the Lord. Live as children of light (for the fruit of the light consists in all goodness, righteousness and truth)* (Eph. 5:8-9). Help us to shine out in this world because we don't support those who are against You.

For You have asked us, *What fellowship can light have with darkness?* (2 Cor. 6:14). May our family shine because we genuinely love others.

For You have said, *Whoever loves his brother lives in the light* (1 John 2:10).

In all these ways, Morning Star, may our family shine for You! Amen.

**TRUTH TO GO**
God wants me to be a star for Him.
(Phil. 2:16)

# 54 | Okay, I'm Convinced!

*No, in all these things we are more than conquerors through him who loved us. For I am convinced that neither death nor life, neither angels nor demons, neither the present nor the future, nor any powers, neither height nor depth, nor anything else in all creation, will be able to separate us from the love of God that is in Christ Jesus our Lord.*

ROMANS 8:37-39

How easy are you to convince? Do you always believe the weather forecast? Or every commercial on TV? It's good not to believe everything you hear. But Paul wanted to make sure Christians always believed in God's love. He wanted them to be *completely convinced, permanently persuaded, absolutely sure, definitely positive* that nothing could separate them from God's love! He wrote to Christians who were being thrown in jail or killed for their beliefs. Even in terrible times, Paul wanted them to be *convinced* that God cared.

### FAMILY TALK

- Why is it important to be totally sure that you can count on God's love? What mistakes could we make if we doubt His love for us?
- Write down on paper three things that make you feel separated from God's love. Then burn them up or throw them away. Then tell God, "I'm convinced! Nothing can separate me from Your love!"

### GOOD NEWS

In the book of Acts, which disciple met and convinced an Ethiopian of the good news of Jesus? (Acts 8:26-40)

# Praying Romans 8 Together

Dear Loving Lord,

Today we are joyfully and completely *convinced* about the one thing that matters most: Your love! We are convinced that neither death nor life, neither angels nor demons, not illness or accidents, not violence or any dark fear can separate our family from Your Love. *For great is Your love toward us, and the faithfulness of the LORD endures forever. Praise the LORD* (from Ps. 117:2).

We are convinced that neither the present nor the future, nor any powers—be they big worries, bad grades, or any principal, judge, president, or king—can separate any of us from Your love! *For You are the faithful God, keeping Your covenant of love to a thousand generations of those who love You and keep Your commands* (from Deut. 7:9).

We are convinced today that neither height nor depth, nor anything else in all creation—not happy days or miserable days, not being rich or being poor, not missing kittens or broken bikes or mean friends or anything else we can think of—will be able to separate our family from the love of God that we have received through Christ Jesus our Lord! Thank You, Lord!

Amen.

**TRUTH TO GO**
Nothing can separate me from God's love.
(Rom. 8:38-39)

# 55 | All Wet

*But I will establish my covenant with you, and you will enter the ark—you
and your sons and your wife and your sons' wives with you. You are to bring
into the ark two of all living creatures, male and female, to keep them alive
with you.... And Noah and his sons and his wife and his sons' wives entered
the ark to escape the waters of the flood.... And rain fell on the earth forty
days and forty nights.*

GENESIS 6:18-19; 7:7,12

When you're all crammed into a car together on a very long trip, it's
easy to get tired and cranky. But think about Noah's family—they were
stuck on a boat for forty days of rain and a hundred more of waiting.
The ark wasn't a cruise ship either. Noah's family had to share space
with noisy, messy, smelly birds and animals.

When hard times hit, we can feel as if they will never end. It's easy
to start picking on each other. But God asks us to hold on and to trust
His promises no matter how long troubles rain down. Soon we'll see
blue skies again.

### FAMILY TALK

- What can God teach us through trials that seem to go on and
  on?
- Has your family ever been stuck in a car or tent or motel room
  for longer than you wanted? What did you do to make time go
  faster?

### COLOR THIS!

The Bible says that all people on earth descended from
Noah's three sons. Can you name them? (Gen. 9:18)

# Praying the Bible Together

Dear Lord,

Thank You for the example of Noah and his family whom You blessed for their patience and faith during a very long, uncomfortable boat ride.

When hard times rain down on our family, fill us with Your Spirit, because "the fruit of the Spirit...is patience" (Gal. 5:22).

Help us to trust Your plans for our future, even if nothing seems to be getting better as far as we can see, because You have told us: "Do not throw away your confidence; it will be richly rewarded. You need to persevere so that when you have done the will of God, you will receive what He has promised" (Heb. 10:35-36).

Thank You that You are good to those whose hope is in You. "It is good to wait quietly for the salvation of the LORD" (Lam. 3:26). Help us all hang on so that Your promises will be fulfilled and You can bless generations to come through our family.

Amen.

**TRUTH TO GO**

When troubles rain down, I won't give up.

(Heb. 10:35)

# 56 | Talk to God...Anytime, Anywhere

*[Jesus] went up into the hills by himself to pray.*

MATTHEW 14:23, NLT

Jesus had just had a very long day. He had walked miles, taught and healed lots of people, then treated a crowd of thousands to a miracle meal! Now He wanted to pray...so He climbed a hill to be by Himself.

Even though Jesus was God, when He wanted to get His strength back, *He prayed!* The Bible tells us of many times when Jesus prayed:

- He prayed when He woke up (Mark 1:35).
- He prayed when He was alone (Luke 5:16).
- He prayed before a meal (Matt. 14:19).
- He prayed when He was feeling upset (John 12:27).
- He prayed in the middle of a crowd (Matt. 19:13).
- He prayed while He was dying on the cross (Matt. 27:46).

For a Christian, praying is talking and listening to our Heavenly Father. If we want to keep alive spiritually, we need to keep praying! In fact, the Bible tells us to "pray continually" (1 Thess. 5:17).

### FAMILY TALK

- When is the best time of day for you to pray?
- When would be a good time to pray that you haven't tried yet?

### A FAMOUS GARDEN

What was the name of the garden where Jesus took His friends to pray? (Mark 14:32)

# Praying the Bible Together

Dear Heavenly Father,

We know that prayer is just talking and listening to You. Thank You for reminding us that You are always ready to listen and help us.

Your Word says, "The LORD is near to all who call on him" (Ps. 145:18).

Thank You, Father, for never being too busy or making us wait while You listen to someone else. Thank You for listening to us when we're happy, grateful, sad, angry, or in any kind of trouble.

Your Word says, "Call upon me in the day of trouble; I will deliver you, and you will honor me" (Ps. 50:15).

Thank You, Heavenly Father, that You will answer our prayer for wisdom if we're having a hard time making a decision.

Your Word says, "Call to me and I will answer you and tell you great and unsearchable things you do not know" (Jer. 33:3).

Thank You so much, Father, that we can just talk!

In Jesus' name. Amen.

**TRUTH TO GO**
Pray all the time.
(1 Thess. 5:17)

# 57 | Listen Up!

*He who answers before listening—that is his folly and his shame.*

PROVERBS 18:13

*My dear brothers, take note of this: Everyone should be quick to listen, slow to speak and slow to become angry.*

JAMES 1:19

Some people say the reason we have only one mouth but two ears is because listening is more important than talking. But it sure is harder, isn't it? Almost all of us are in a hurry to say what we want to say, and we forget to listen.

The Bible says that answering before listening is foolish. That's because a good listener can follow directions and answer questions better. Good listeners are smart *and* well-liked. No wonder God wants us to close our mouths and open up our ears!

### FAMILY TALK

- Take a vote to determine who is the best listener in your family. Why did you choose the one you did? Ask that person for tips on good listening.
- What is the difference between listening and hearing? Talk about different ways you can show someone you're really listening.

### "IS THAT YOU, LORD?"

What young boy had a hard time believing what he was hearing in the middle of the night?
(1 Sam. 3:1-10)

# Praying the Bible Together

Dear Lord,
Please forgive us for all the times we're bad listeners.
Instead of being quick to hear,
we race to speak (James 1:19).
Thank You that Your ears
are never closed to our prayers (Isa. 59:1).
Make us more like You, Lord!
When we need to know the truth
or when one of us is hurting,
give us ears that really listen (Matt.11:15).
When we are tempted to criticize,
help us to stop—and try to praise instead (Prov. 10:19).
We really do want to change, Lord!
And we want to start today by listening to You.
We say with Samuel, "Speak, LORD,
for your servant is listening" (1 Sam. 3:9).
Amen.

**TRUTH TO GO**
Be slow to speak, quick to listen.
(James 1:19)

# 58 | Not Guilty!

*Who is he that condemns? Christ Jesus, who died—more than that, who was raised to life—is at the right hand of God and is also interceding for us.*

ROMANS 8:34

If you haven't visited a courtroom during a trial, you've probably seen one on TV. Since the Roman Empire was proud of its legal system, Paul used courtroom language to help people understand what their salvation meant.

Think of how you became a Christian as a trial scene: You were guilty of sin and deserved to be called up to the witness stand to be tried. Satan was your accuser. But just as you were about to be found guilty and sentenced to die, Jesus came through the courtroom door. He came not just to plead your cause but to take your place! He startled the courtroom with an amazing announcement. "I've already paid the price for all the sins in question—past, present, and future. So let the accused go free. Because I took the penalty of his sins, he must be pardoned and released!"

## FAMILY TALK

➥ What's the difference between being pardoned and being innocent?

➥ What should you do when you feel guilty about something you've done?

## RANSOM PRICE

Who gave His life in exchange for our freedom? (1 Tim. 2:5-6)

# Praying the Bible Together

Dear Heavenly Father,

Thank You that You loved the world so much that You sent Your only Son, Jesus, so that anyone in this family who believes in Him will be saved from sin and given eternal life (John 3:16)!

We know Father, that our righteousness is borrowed from Jesus, who was perfect in every way. Your Word says:

> He saved us, not because of righteous things we had
> done, but because of his mercy. He saved us through
> the washing of rebirth and renewal by the Holy
> Spirit, whom he poured out on us generously
> through Jesus Christ our Savior, so that having been
> justified by his grace, we might become heirs hav-
> ing the hope of eternal life. (Titus 3:5-7)

Thank You that through Jesus, we will never be found guilty. Instead we are forgiven (Rom. 3:24-25), clean (1 Cor. 6:11), and free (Gal. 5:1). Through Jesus we have new life and power for every day (1 John 5:12) and eternal life waiting for us in heaven (John 3:36).

Thank You that "if anyone is in Christ, he is a new creation; the old has gone, the new has come!" (2 Cor. 5:17).

Amen!

**TRUTH TO GO**
Jesus makes me new all through!
(2 Cor. 5:17)

# 59 | Pass the Salt, Please

*Let your conversation be always full of grace, seasoned with salt, so that you may know how to answer everyone.*

COLOSSIANS 4:6

In his letter to Christians in the city of Colosse, Paul said they should sprinkle their words with salt. Sounds weird, doesn't it? But salt was almost as valuable as silver in those days. They used it as money to trade for important things. They used it to stay healthy. They used salt to make food taste better and to make it last longer (remember, they didn't have refrigerators).

That's why Paul told them to season their words with salt. He meant, "Make your words pleasant. Make your conversations valuable." Jesus said that Christians were like salt—we share His goodness with everyone we meet.

So, pass the salt, please! Let's sprinkle our words with good flavor.

### FAMILY TALK

- What kind of words would "taste" good to others?
- Can you think of someone who seems sad or angry and needs to hear some kindness or encouragement?
- Make it a dinner rule for the week: Every time you salt your food, you have to compliment someone at the table!

### RUB·A·DUB·DUB

What wiggly wonders were rubbed in salt for good health in Bible times? (Ezek. 16:4)

# Praying the Bible Together

Dear Lord of our family,

Thank You for this encouragement today from Your Word to use words only that help others. You want our words to encourage. You want us to say the right words at the right time.

You've asked us to do these things with our words:

- to say no bad things about others (Titus 3:2)
- to say only what is good and helpful (Eph. 4:29)
- to speak the truth with love (Eph. 4:15)
- to always be ready to tell others about Jesus (1 Pet. 3:15)

Help us to season our conversations with Your grace today. Amen.

**TRUTH TO GO**

Fill my words with good flavor.

(Col. 4:6)

# 60 | Judas's Big Mistake

*When Judas, who had betrayed him, saw that Jesus was condemned, he was seized with remorse and returned the thirty silver coins to the chief priests and the elders. "I have sinned," he said, "for I have betrayed innocent blood."*

MATTHEW 27:3-4

Judas was one of Jesus' twelve most trusted disciples. He had spent three years learning from Jesus and serving Him. Then he turned traitor. What happened? Was he trying to force Jesus to choose to be a political leader instead of just a spiritual one? Did he expect that Jesus would do a miracle and rescue Himself? No one knows for sure.

When Judas saw that Jesus was condemned to die, he didn't even wait for a miracle. He was so sorry for betraying his friend that he went away and hanged himself. He must have been sure Jesus could never forgive him for what he had done. That was Judas's biggest mistake.

### FAMILY TALK

- To betray means to help the enemy instead of a friend. Have you ever been betrayed by a friend? Were you able to forgive?
- Admitting a wrong and feeling regret are the first steps to making things right. But if you want to fully repent, what else should you do?

### BETRAYAL TIMES THREE

Another disciple turned against Jesus by saying three times that he'd never even heard of Him. Who was he? (Mark 14:66-72)

# Praying the Bible Together

Dear Heavenly Father,

Today we are thankful that You are a forgiving God. The Bible promises: "You are forgiving and good, O Lord, abounding in love to all who call to you" (Ps. 86:5).

We love You because You are kind and merciful. Help us never to run away from You when we've done something wrong, as Judas did, but to run toward You, as Peter did, and ask You for forgiveness. No matter what we've done, or how bad we feel about it, the Bible promises: "If we confess our sins, he is faithful and just and will forgive us our sins and purify us from all unrighteousness" (1 John 1:9).

Keep us from betrayals of all kinds—from turning against You, from not doing what we say we will, from hurting people we love. Thank You that we don't have to live with regret and fear. We can always find forgiveness and a clean conscience again. Your Word promises: "Godly sorrow brings repentance that leads to salvation and leaves no regret" (2 Cor 7:10).

Amen.

**TRUTH TO GO**
If I confess, He will forgive.
(1 John 1:9)

# 61 | Abba, Father

*How great is the love the Father has lavished on us, that we should be called children of God! And that is what we are!*

1 JOHN 3:1

Up until the time Jesus came to earth, no one would have dreamed of calling God, "Daddy." The Jewish people saw God as powerful and loving—but only to be approached with great reverence. They were even afraid to say or write God's name. But Jesus called God, "Abba" (Mark 14:36). In the language that Jesus spoke, "Abba" is a word kids used at home—it means "Dad" or "Daddy."

When you ask Jesus to be your Savior, you become part of God's family. That means you are children of "Abba, Father," and Christ is your brother.

Because Jesus came, all of us can call God "Daddy" if we want to. He won't be angry. Instead, our Heavenly Father will pick us up in His arms and love us.

### FAMILY TALK

- What comes to mind when you think of the word "Daddy"? How does it feel to call God by this name?
- What do parents and God have in common? What is different about them?

### FATHER OF ISRAEL

Who did the Jews refer to as their father? (John 8:31-41)

# Praying the Bible Together

(Read these verse prayers aloud, inserting the name of a family member in each.)

Thank You, Heavenly Father, for Your love!
How great is the love that You have lavished on _____, that he/she should be called "a child of God." And that's exactly what he/she is (from 1 John 3:1)!

Dear Father,
We praise You that because _____ has believed Jesus Christ and accepted Him, the Lord has given _____ the right to become a child of God (from John 1:12).

O God,
Thank You that You sent Your Son that _____ might receive the full rights of a son or daughter. Because _____ is Your child, Your Spirit in his/her heart can call out, "Abba, Father!" And since _____ is now Your child, he/she is also an heir of God (from Gal. 4:4-7).

**TRUTH TO GO**
My Father loves me!
(1 John 3:1)

# 62 | On with the Show!

*I tell you the truth, you are looking for me, not because you saw miraculous signs but because you ate the loaves and had your fill.*

JOHN 6:26

Jesus performed many miracles—the Bible records thirty-four! These were events where God's power made normally impossible things happen. Jesus walked on water, He calmed a storm, He fed thousands with one lunch, and He healed the sick. He even brought dead people back to life.

Many people today say, "I'd believe in God if I saw a miracle." But seeing miracles didn't lead people to repent and follow Jesus' teaching. They only wanted more miracles. "Show us a sign!" they begged (Matt. 16:1). What they really meant was, "Put on a show, Jesus! Entertain us!"

Jesus wants us to follow Him, not just because of what He can do but because we believe in Him and love Him!

### FAMILY TALK

- Have you ever had people hang around you only so they could get something from you that they wanted? How did that make you feel?
- If you saw a man walk on water or raise the dead, do you think you would change how you live? Would you follow him as God?

### WAY DEAD!

How long had Lazarus been buried when Jesus brought him back to life? (John 11:38–40)

# Praying the Bible Together

Dear Jesus,
You can make blind people see (Mark 7:32-35).
And You can help lame men walk (Mark 2:3-12).
You can stop the wind (Matt. 8:26).
And You can walk on water (Matt. 14:25).
You can heal the sick (John 4:46-53).
And You can bring the dead back to life (John 11:17-44).
You can turn water into wine for a wedding
    (John 2:6-10).
And You can turn one boy's snack into a feast
    (John 6:8-13).
Best of all, You can save me from my sins (Acts 4:12).
You can make me a new person inside (2 Cor. 5:17).
You can do miracles for others through me
    (John 14:12).
And You can make me live forever (John 3:16).
Yes, You are a God of miracles.
So I praise You today for Your power.
And even more—I love You just for being You!
Amen.

**TRUTH TO GO**
I trust Jesus for His power
and love Him for His person.
(John 6:26)

# 63 | Battling Giants

*David said to the Philistine, "You come against me with sword and spear and javelin, but I come against you in the name of the LORD Almighty, the God of the armies of Israel.... The battle is the LORD's." As the Philistine moved closer to attack him, David ran quickly toward the battle line to meet him. Reaching into his bag and taking out a stone, he slung it and struck the Philistine on the forehead. The stone sank into his forehead, and he fell facedown on the ground. So David triumphed over the Philistine with a sling and a stone.*

1 SAMUEL 17:45-50

While Saul and the Israelites looked at the warrior-giant named Goliath, they were "dismayed and terrified" (1 Sam. 17:11). But David, a young shepherd boy, spoke with great confidence, predicting his victory and the giant's defeat.

What made David so brave? He trusted in the Lord, not in himself. "I come against you in the name of the LORD Almighty," he shouted. The young boy with a slingshot proved that when we put our trust in God, we can take on even giants and win!

### FAMILY TALK

- Can you remember a time when you faced a scary problem or opponent that seemed as big as Goliath to you? How did it turn out?
- What are some spiritual weapons that God gives us to help us win against wrong influences? (Eph. 6:10-18)

### THE MEASURE OF A GIANT

How many feet tall was Goliath? (1 Sam. 17:4)

# Praying the Bible Together

Heavenly Father,
David was able to win over a giant because
he relied on You and not himself.
We want to do the same because:
*The battle is the Lord's* (1 Sam. 17:47).
Each day when one of us is facing something
way too big and scary to handle alone,
help us to remember:
*The battle is the Lord's.*
Whenever others are speaking against you, Lord,
we will stand up to them, because we know:
*The battle is the Lord's.*
Thank You that when we face giants of any kind,
You will help us to gain victory
so that we can tell everybody:
*The battle is the Lord's!*
Amen.

**TRUTH TO GO**
The battle is the Lord's!
(1 Sam. 17:47)

# 64 | Angels Watching over Me

*Are not all angels ministering spirits sent to serve those who will inherit salvation?*

HEBREWS 1:14

Angels are popular in books, paintings, and on top of Christmas trees. Pictures show them fat and friendly or ghostly and mysterious. But what are they really like?

Angels are heavenly beings created by God to serve Him on earth and worship Him in heaven. They don't have physical bodies as we do, but they are very powerful. Angels defend us against danger and evil powers. Sometimes they deliver important messages for God.

On Christmas trees and in storybooks, angels usually look as pretty as, well, an angel. But they must be frightening, too. People in the Bible who were visited by an angel usually felt afraid. How do we know? Because the first words the angels spoke was nearly always, "Fear not!"

## FAMILY TALK

↪ Many people believe they have a special guardian angel assigned to keep an eye on them, help them avoid trouble or accidents, nudge them onto the right path. Have you ever felt as if you had one of these angels? Why or why not?

↪ Would you like to see an angel, or would you be afraid?

## TOUCHED BY AN ANGEL

Only two of God's angels are named in Scripture. Who are they? (Luke 1:26-38; Rev. 12:7-12)

# Praying the Bible Together

Lord of Angels,

Thank You for surrounding our family with Your heavenly beings. How good it is to know that these powerful guardians defend us in ways that we can't see or understand (Eph. 6:12).

Thank You for the reminder today that angels are ministering spirits sent to serve us, because we have inherited Your salvation (Heb. 1:14). Thank You that Your angel warriors can do so many things for us:

- shut the mouths of lions (Dan. 6:22)
- protect us from enemies like Satan (Ps. 34:7)
- save us from dangers that we can't see (Ps. 91:9-12)

Lord, You said that even the smallest child in this family has an angel in heaven who is always serving in Your presence (Matt. 18:10).

When any of us is afraid today, help us to remember our angels. And help us to behave like angels too—to serve You and worship You with every ounce of our energy!

Amen.

**TRUTH TO GO**
Angels watch over me.
(Ps. 91:11)

# 65 | Out of the Lion's Mouth

*At the first light of dawn, the king got up and hurried to the lions' den. When he came near the den, he called to Daniel in an anguished voice, "Daniel, servant of the living God, has your God, whom you serve continually, been able to rescue you from the lions?" Daniel answered, "O king, live forever! My God sent his angel, and he shut the mouths of the lions. They have not hurt me, because I was found innocent in his sight. Nor have I ever done any wrong before you, O king."*

DANIEL 6:19-21

Remember the story of Daniel and the lions' den? Some evil politicians who hated Daniel set a trap for him. They knew he was King Darius's favorite advisor. They also knew he prayed to God every day. So they got the king to sign a law that said everyone had to pray to him, not to any other person or god.

Even though Daniel knew the law was a trap, he continued to pray to God three times a day. He even prayed with his window open so others could see him. Daniel's enemies arrested him and threw him into the lions' den. Then they left, sure that he would soon be dead. But they forgot that God could shut the mouths of the lions!

### FAMILY TALK

- ↝ Daniel was willing to put his life in jeopardy just to pray to his God. Do you think he was sure God would save him?
- ↝ Take a minute to pray for Christians who are in jail or are suffering in other ways for their faith.

### "GOTCHA!"

What Bible hero killed a lion with his bare hands? (Judg. 14:5-6)

# Praying Psalm 91 Together

Almighty God,
You are our refuge and fortress;
we trust in You (v. 2)!
You have promised to keep us safe;
Your faithfulness will be our shield (vv. 3-4).
Thank You, Almighty God!
You say we don't need to fear anything—
terrors at night,
attacks during the day,
or sickness (vv. 5-6).
Thank You, Almighty God!
You promise to protect us
as You did Daniel.
Your Word says:

> "He will command his angels concerning you
> to guard you in all your ways" (v. 11).

Thank You, Almighty God!
You are very strong.
We trust You, and we love You!
Amen.

**TRUTH TO GO**
God will keep me safe.
(Ps. 91:4)

# 66 | Juvenile Delinquent

*The woman gave birth to a boy and named him Samson. He grew and the LORD blessed him, and the Spirit of the LORD began to stir him.*

JUDGES 13:24-25

*One day Samson went to Gaza, where he saw a prostitute. He went in to spend the night with her.*

JUDGES 16:1

God chose Samson for a very special job—to lead Israel to victory over their enemies, the Philistines. Samson never cut his hair as a reminder of what he was supposed to do. God gave him incredible strength (once he killed a thousand enemy soldiers all by himself). But even his long hair couldn't keep Samson from forgetting God's plan. Instead of fighting Israel's enemies, he used to go to their cities, like Gaza, to play and buy sexual favors. What a fool!

Samson has been called the Bible's most famous juvenile delinquent. Like a movie star who lets fame go to his head, Samson became foolish and arrogant. As a result, he lost his strength and died as a prisoner of his enemies.

### FAMILY TALK

- Decide together what special gifts or talents God has given every family member. How could you use them for God? How could you waste them?
- Do you think special talents are always inherited from a parent?

### SAMSON THE BARBARIAN

What animal bone did Samson use to defeat an army? (Judg. 15:15-16)

# Praying the Bible Together

Dear Heavenly Father,

Help us to learn from Samson's mistakes. We want to grow up and get wiser and stronger every day! Teach us to love common sense more than a thrill. Help us never to play with danger or tease ourselves with temptation. Keep us away from drugs, alcohol, the wrong friends, and every immoral choice.

Father, You've set aside every person in this family for a noble purpose (2 Tim. 2:20-21). You will give us special strength to make it happen. Thank You that—if we cooperate with You, You will complete the good thing You've already begun in our lives (Phil. 1:6)!

Instead of following temptations, help us to run away from evil desires. Help us to "pursue righteousness, faith, love and peace, along with those who call on You out of a pure heart" (from 2 Tim. 2:22).

With Your help, God, we know we don't have to make the same dumb mistakes again and again. We can "become mature in our understanding, as strong Christians ought to be" (Heb. 6:1, TLB). We can be faithful, mighty champions for You. And that's what we want too.

In Jesus' name. Amen.

**TRUTH TO GO**
God wants me to grow up!
(Heb. 6:1)

# 67 | Ten to Keep, Part 1

*Keep his decrees and commands...so that it may go well with you and your children after you.*

DEUTERONOMY 4:40

God decided that His people, the Jews (also called the Israelites), needed a clear set of rules to show them how to live well and please Him. So God sent Moses to the top of a mountain. There God told Moses His laws. He told him to write down everything on stone tablets, which Moses did. Then Moses brought them to the Israelites and taught them what God had said. Obeying God's laws would bring blessing, Moses said. Disobedience would bring a curse.

Today we call these laws of God the Ten Commandments. When we follow them, we please God and make our own lives better too.

### FAMILY TALK

↰ Talk through the first five commandments (see Exod. 20). How do they apply to your family? Command 1: You shall have no other gods. Command 2: You shall not make idols. Command 3: You shall not misuse the name of God. Command 4: You shall keep the Sabbath holy. Command 5: You shall honor your father and mother.

### STAGE FRIGHT

Even though he was Israel's leader, Moses didn't like to speak in public. So his brother did a lot of the talking for him. What was the brother's name? (Exod. 4:10-17)

# Praying the Ten Commandments Together, Part 1

Lord God,

Show our family what it means to fear You and keep Your laws. You said: "I am the LORD your God.... You shall have no other gods before me" (Deut. 5:6-7). May no other loyalties or priority take Your place in our hearts!

You said: "You shall not make for yourself an idol in the form of anything in heaven or on earth. You shall not worship them, for I am a jealous God" (from 5:8-9). Help us to turn away from all wrong beliefs and to not worship anything or anyone but You.

You said: "You shall not misuse the name of the LORD your God" (5:11). Help us to always honor Your name. May we only say "Lord," "God," and "Jesus Christ" when we mean it respectfully and sincerely.

You said: "Observe the Sabbath day by keeping it holy" (5:12). May we faithfully set aside the Lord's day for church, rest, and family times.

You said: "Honor your father and your mother, as the LORD your God has commanded you, so that you may live long and that it may go well with you" (5:16). Help the kids in this family to respect and obey Mom and Dad as You've asked. And we will look for Your blessings as a result.

Amen.

**TRUTH TO GO**
Obey God's commandments.
(Deut. 4:40)

# 68 | Ten to Keep, Part 2

*Take care to follow the commandments, decrees and laws I give you today. If you pay attention to these laws and are careful to follow them, then the LORD your God will keep his covenant of love with you, as he swore to your forefathers.*

DEUTERONOMY 7:11-12

God tells us over and over again how important it is for us to obey His commandments. In the verses above, notice these words: "pay attention," "take care," and "careful." But maybe most important is the little word "if." God promised His people that *if* they obeyed each law carefully and completely, *then* He would keep His promise to bring them all His blessings. Unlike the Hebrew people who first heard these rules, today we have the Holy Spirit's power to help us obey God's commandments—and Jesus to forgive us when we fail.

### FAMILY TALK

↞ How do the next five commandments apply to your family— kids as well as parents? Command 6: You shall not murder. Command 7: You shall not commit adultery (sexual sin). Command 8: You shall not steal. Command 9: You shall not give false testimony. Command 10: You shall not covet (want what doesn't belong to you).

↞ Which of them seems hardest for you to follow?

### ON THE OTHER SIDE

After the Israelites received the commandments, what river did they need to cross to reach the Promised Land? (Deut. 6:1)

# Praying the Ten Commandments Together, Part 2

Dear Lord,

We want to worship You in our home today by keeping Your commands in how we think and what we do. You said: "You shall not murder" (5:17). Help our family to protect all human life—including unborn babies and the very old or ill. May we never, even in our thoughts, hurt people with hatred, violence, or revenge.

You said: "You shall not commit adultery" (5:18). Help us always to respect members of the opposite sex and treat them with purity. May we honor marriage as a lifelong covenant.

You said: "You shall not steal" (5:19). Teach us to respect the belongings of others, and to trust You, our Provider, to take care of all our wants and needs.

You said: "You shall not give false testimony against your neighbor" (5:20). May we never lie, tattle, spread false rumors, or say unkind things about others.

You said: "You shall not covet" (5:21). Help us to be content with what You give us. When others have more or succeed, help us to be happy for them.

Thank You, Lord, that as we follow Your commands You will give us the very best life possible!

Amen.

**TRUTH TO GO**
The Ten Commandments are one great idea!
(Deut. 7:12)

# 69 | A Barn Full of Surprises

*While they were there, the time came for the baby to be born, and she gave birth to her firstborn, a son. She wrapped him in cloths and placed him in a manger, because there was no room for them in the inn.*

LUKE 2:6-7

Have you ever been in a Christmas play? Maybe you were a shepherd with a brown painted beard, or a beautiful angel with pretty foil wings. But the real manger scene was not so pretty. It was probably cold, damp, and smelly. Joseph must have been pretty upset. His young wife was about to give birth to the Son of God—and he couldn't even find her a bed!

God's plans for all of us are usually full of surprises. That's because when things don't go the way we expect or we don't know what to do, God has a chance to show us more of His power and love.

### FAMILY TALK

➤ When shepherds arrived at the stable and told Joseph, "Angels appeared to us and told us about your new baby, Jesus!" how do you think he felt? Shocked? Worried? Relieved?

➤ What do you think he learned about God's surprises?

### O LITTLE TOWN
What town was Jesus born in? (Luke 2:4-7)

# Praying the Bible Together

Dear Heavenly Father,

Thank You so much for sending Your Son, Jesus Christ, to be born in a stable. What a surprising way to send a Savior into the world! We ask You to help us to be ready for Your surprises—at school, at home, with our friends. When things seem out of control, help us to trust that You are still in control.

We admit, God, that we'll never really understand how You think or plan our lives. In the Bible, You tell us: "My thoughts are not your thoughts, neither are your ways my ways.… As the heavens are higher than the earth, so are my ways higher than your ways and my thoughts than your thoughts" (Isa. 55:8-9).

Thank You that You are always at work—in every challenge, in every surprise, in every mistake, in everything that happens—to accomplish good for Your children. Your Word promises: "All things work together for good to them that love God, to them who are the called according to his purpose" (Rom. 8:28, KJV).

When challenges strike, send us encouragement, as You did for Joseph and Mary, to let us know that we are where You want us to be.

Amen.

**TRUTH TO GO**
God's ways are not my ways.
(Isa. 55:8)

# 70 | Whose Turn for Dishes?

*Whatever you do, work at it with all your heart, as working for the Lord, not for men.*

COLOSSIANS 3:23

It takes a whole family working together to keep a home running right and looking good. We all have to keep our rooms clean, pick up our own messes, and do chores like helping with the dishes. The Bible is full of examples of people who worked hard to help others:

- Noah worked for years to build an ark to keep his family safe (Gen. 6).
- Jacob herded sheep for fourteen years to earn the right to marry Rachel (Gen. 29:1-30).
- Ruth went every day to the fields to find leftover grain so she and her mother-in-law could eat (Ruth 2).
- Jesus washed the dusty, smelly feet of all twelve of His disciples to show them how much He loved them (John 13:4-5).

Suddenly doing the dishes doesn't sound so bad!

### FAMILY TALK

- How are chores assigned in your house? Is someone carrying too much of the load? What can you do to help?
- When you do a chore as if you're doing it for Jesus, how does it change the experience?

### LAZY BONES

"Lazy hands make a man _____." (Prov. 10:4)

# Praying the Bible Together

Dear Lord,

It's a lie that good things happen without effort. Or by letting someone else do the work. Or just by talking about what needs to happen but not doing anything about it. The Bible teaches us that You always bless us when we work hard. But it also says that laziness of any kind leads to disgrace, poverty, and unhappiness (Prov. 10:4; 12:24; 13:4).

Please, Lord, we want to be a family that works together like a team. Help us to be willing to do our chores without complaining. Help us to be the first to volunteer when something needs to be done.

Help us to remember these verses today:

"Do everything without complaining or arguing" (Phil. 2:14)

and

"Whatever you do, work at it with all your heart, as working for the Lord, not for men.... It is the Lord Christ you are serving" (Col. 3:23-24).

Amen.

**TRUTH TO GO**

Whatever I do, I'll do for the Lord with all my heart.
(Col. 3:23)

# 71 | Praise the Lord!

*Praise the LORD. Praise, the LORD, O my soul. I will praise the LORD all my life; I will sing praise to my God as long as I live.*

PSALM 146:1-2

When you do something right at school, your teacher praises you. When you hit the ball out of the park, your coach says, "Way to go! You're awesome!" When you take first place in a contest, the crowd claps for you. And who doesn't like getting the praise they deserve!

It's important to praise the Lord for the same reason. God does everything perfectly every day. So it's only right to tell Him so! The Bible says, "It is good to praise the LORD and make music to your name, O Most High, to proclaim your love in the morning and your faithfulness at night" (Ps. 92:1).

When we praise God through music or words, we remind ourselves and everyone else around, "God did this! He's wonderful!"

## FAMILY TALK

↪ Different people praise God in different ways. Different churches use different styles of worship. What kinds of praise do you like best? Do you think God only wants one kind of praise?

↪ Sing your favorite song or say your favorite verse that worships God.

## NEVER TOO YOUNG

"From the lips of _____ and _____ you have ordained praise." (Ps. 8:2)

# Praying Psalm 145 Together

O God, our King,
Great are You, Lord, and most worthy of praise. Your greatness no one can even understand (v. 3). That's why our family says right now,
*Every day we will praise you* (v. 2).

One generation in our family will praise Your works to the next. We will celebrate Your kindness. We will sing about Your goodness (vv. 4,7).
*Every day we will praise you.*

You are so kind. You are always slow to get angry. You are rich in love (v. 8).
*Every day we will praise you.*

You, O Lord, are faithful to do everything You have promised. You are loving toward everything You have made (v. 13).
*Every day we will praise you.*

You lift us up when we fall. You give us food when we're hungry (vv. 14-16).
*Every day we will praise you.*

You hear us when we pray; You understand our secret cries (vv.18-19).
*Every day we will praise you.*

Praise the Lord!
Amen.

**TRUTH TO GO**
Every day I will praise you.
(Ps. 145:2)

# 72 | "Dear World..."

*You yourselves are our letter, written on our hearts, known and read by everybody. You...are a letter from Christ, the result of our ministry, written not with ink but with the Spirit of the living God, not on tablets of stone but on tablets of human hearts.*

2 CORINTHIANS 3:2-3

In Paul's time (two thousand years ago), there were no phones or postal service. People communicated with friends in distant places by letters that were hand-delivered by messengers. In these verses, Paul told Christians that they themselves were like a letter to the world from Christ. Paul meant that what we do and say is like a letter that other people read to learn about Jesus.

### FAMILY TALK

- Sometimes you might want to keep your life sealed up in an envelope where no one can read it. What would make you feel that way?
- Since we're each a letter to the world from Christ, decide what one thing you most want your non-Christian friends to "read" today.

### LETTERS TO ONE

Four of Paul's thirteen letters in the New Testament went to individuals, not to churches. Name them.

# Praying the Bible Together

Dear Lord Jesus,
We thank You today
that You are up to something grand in this family!
You're still writing good news to our world,
and the good news is us—
our words,
our actions,
our attitudes.
Remind us throughout the day
that we're being opened
and read
and remembered
by people who need to know about You.
May every word of our "letters"
be full of encouragement
and truth
and love.
In Jesus' name we pray. Amen.

**TRUTH TO GO**
My life is Jesus' letter to the world.
(2 Cor. 3:2-3)

# 73 | Two for the Road

*Now that same day [the day Jesus rose from the dead] two [disciples] were going to a village called Emmaus, about seven miles from Jerusalem. They were talking with each other about everything that had happened. As they talked and discussed these things with each other, Jesus himself came up and walked along with them; but they were kept from recognizing him.*

LUKE 24:13-16

Two very sad men were walking on a road. Their friend and teacher, Jesus, had been crucified only a few days before. Now he was dead and buried. For these two men, all their hopes were dead and buried too.

Then a third man joined them. It was Jesus, but they were so discouraged and sad, they didn't really see who it was. Mile after mile the two sad men kept talking. They told the third man everything that had happened. They told him how sad they were.

Then the third man started teaching them from the Bible. He said that their friend Jesus had come to earth for a purpose: to die—and to rise again! Filled with hope, they suddenly recognized who was talking to them. It was Jesus Himself! And He was alive!

### FAMILY TALK

- Have you ever been so upset or sad about something that you stopped noticing what was going on around you? What had gone wrong?
- How can reading the Bible help you get the right perspective?

### LOOK AGAIN

Who also didn't recognize Jesus standing next to her until He said her name? (John 20:15-16)

# Praying the Bible Together

Dear Lord Jesus,

We're so glad You were raised up from the dead! We're so glad You're alive today!

Lord Jesus, walk with us when we're discouraged or sad, when nothing seems to make sense, when we've given up hope, when we've lost our way. Walk with us and talk with us. Speak to our hearts, Jesus, as You did to your sad and lonely friends.

When we open the Bible, let us hear Your voice. As we read about Your life, show us how to live. As we read Psalms, show us how to praise You and be thankful. As we read Proverbs, give us Your wisdom. Let Your voice burn in our hearts as it did for those men on the road to Emmaus.

We want to know it's You—only You! No one else! When we hear You, we want to say with those two men: "When Jesus talked to us on the road, it felt like a fire burning in us. It was exciting when he explained the true meaning of the Scriptures" (Luke 24:32, ICB).

Please, Jesus, walk and talk with us every day. That's the only way we can really be happy.

Amen.

**TRUTH TO GO**
Jesus walks and talks with me.
(Luke 24:32)

# 74 | Jesus in the Mirror

*And we, who...all reflect the Lord's glory, are being transformed into his likeness.*

2 CORINTHIANS 3:18

Your face isn't an accident, you know! Really! The way you look has been passed down to you from your birth parents and your grandparents before them. Maybe you've got your mother's mouth, your father's chin, or your great-grandma's laugh. It's called "family resemblance."

Once you become a Christian, God wants you to have a family resemblance too. He wants you to look a lot like Jesus. (God means how you look on the inside, not the shape of your nose.) When Jesus comes to live in your heart, you start to look more like Him right away in how you think and act. And a lifetime of asking, "What would Jesus do?"—and then doing it—makes you look more and more like Him.

### FAMILY TALK

- Read the opening verse again. What do key words like "reflect," "transformed," and "likeness" mean? Do you think others see the "likeness" of Jesus in your life?
- Nominate someone you know who "looks" (in words and deeds) a lot like Jesus. What is it about them that sets them apart?

### LOOK-ALIKES?

"So God created man in his own _____, in the _____ of God he created them; male and female he created them." (Gen. 1:27)

# Praying the Bible Together

Heavenly Father,

When You first made the human race, You had in mind that we would look a lot like You. But sin and disobedience really changed the way we look and act. By Your powerful Spirit, Father, make our family more and more like You every day. We want Your beauty on our faces, in our words, in everything we do. Help us to clothe ourselves with the Lord Jesus Christ so that sin doesn't have a chance to make us ugly (Rom. 13:14).

The Bible says:

> Therefore, I urge you, brothers, in view of God's
> mercy, to offer your bodies as living sacrifices, holy
> and pleasing to God.... Do not conform any longer to
> the pattern of this world, but be transformed by the
> renewing of your mind. (Rom. 12:1-2)

Transform us! Change us and shape us more each day, God! By Your power, this will happen as we read Your Word, spend time praying and listening to You, learn from older Christians, and obey You with all our heart.

Heavenly Father, may You always be proud of our "family resemblance" to Your Son.

In His name we pray. Amen.

**TRUTH TO GO**
What would Jesus do?
(John 6:38)

# 75 | Pep Talk

*Find rest, O my soul, in God alone; my hope comes from him.*

PSALM 62:5

*Why are you downcast, O my soul?… Put your hope in God, for I will yet praise him.*

PSALM 42:11

When you're all by yourself and you're trying to figure something out, do you ever talk to yourself? "Let's see," you might say when you're doing your homework, "I think I'll add that number and subtract that one." Or maybe after you fall off your bike, you yell, "How could I be such a klutz!"

In the psalms, David sometimes talked to himself. Look at the verses at the top of this page again. David is giving his soul a pep talk. "Cheer up, Dave!" he says. "God is going to help you out!"

Sometimes we should do the same thing. Why? Because our feelings make us forget what we *know* is true. Even if we feel hopeless, we can still have hope because not even one awesome thing about God has changed!

### FAMILY TALK

- Talk about a situation you faced during the past week where you could have used a pep talk from yourself.
- What truth about God do you need to say out loud?

### REMEMBER THIS

Once, when David was very discouraged, he met a woman who reminded him exactly who he was. Her words kept David from violence. Who was this brave woman he later married? (1 Sam. 25:14-35)

# Praying the Bible Together

Lord,
Today, we put all of our hope in You.
We will speak Your words to our souls,
and we will meditate on them all day long.

> "Find rest, O my soul,
> in God alone;
> my hope comes from him" (Ps. 62:5).
> "Why are you downcast, O my soul?…
> Put your hope in God,
> for I will yet praise him" (Ps. 42:11).
> "We wait in hope for the LORD;
> He is our help and our shield.
> In him our hearts rejoice,
> for we trust in his holy name.
> May Your unfailing love
> rest upon us, O LORD,
> even as we put our hope in you" (Ps. 33:20-22).

Amen.

**TRUTH TO GO**
God is my hope.
(Ps. 62:5)

# 76 | The Hiding Place

*I have hidden your word in my heart, that I might not sin against you.*

PSALM 119:11

What does it mean to "hide" God's Word in your heart? Think about it this way: A dog hides his bone in a special place in the backyard so he can dig it up whenever he needs it. Maybe you hide your diaries or your most valuable collector cards so you're sure no one else will take them.

In the same way, God wants you to read the Bible, think about it, remember it, and love it so you'll never be without it. One good way to hide God's Word in your heart is to memorize verses. That way, when you need to remember something God said, you'll have it right on the tip of your tongue.

## FAMILY TALK

- When the author Corrie ten Boom was put in a concentration camp during World War II, the parts of the Bible she'd memorized brought her encouragement. And she taught other prisoners the verses she knew. If you couldn't have a Bible tomorrow, how much could you remember? What part would you most like to have memorized?

- If you don't have a family Bible memory plan, start with today's verse from Psalm 119. The whole psalm is about the importance of living by God's words.

## RAZOR SHARP

"The word of God is living and active. Sharper than any double-edged _____." (Heb. 4:12)

# Praying the Bible Together

Heavenly Father,

Today we pray that You will help us to keep Bible verses in our thoughts and memories so we'll know how to live for You. You've told us how important Your words are. Today we pray these verses together:

> All Scripture is given by God
> and is useful for teaching
> and for showing people what is wrong in their lives.
> It is useful for correcting faults
> and teaching how to live right.
> Using the Scriptures,
> the person who serves God
> will be ready
> and will have everything he needs
> to do every good work. (2 Tim. 3:16-17, ICB)

Yes, Lord—help us to read and remember Your words. We want to take time to memorize verses too so that they can live in our hearts and make us wiser and draw us closer to You (Col. 3:16).

Amen.

**TRUTH TO GO**
I have hidden God's Word in my heart.
(Ps. 119:11)

# 77 | Someone's Watching over You

*When [Moses' mother] saw that he was a fine child, she hid him for three months. But when she could hide him no longer, she got a papyrus basket for him and coated it with tar and pitch. Then she placed the child in it and put it among the reeds along the bank of the Nile.*

EXODUS 2:2-3

While the Israelites were slaves in Egypt, Pharaoh began to worry that too many baby boys were being born. What if all these boys grew up strong and decided to rebel? So Pharaoh ordered all the midwives (women who help to deliver babies) to kill any Israelite boys that were born (Exod. 1:22).

But when Moses was born, his mother decided to protect him. That's how Baby Moses ended up floating gently in the reeds beside the river. God was watching out for Baby Moses. Pharaoh's own daughter came down to the river to take a bath and found him. She decided to adopt him (Exod. 2:5-10) and even asked his mother to be his nurse!

### FAMILY TALK

- Talk about a time when something bad or scary happened to you or your family. Looking back now, can you see how God was watching over you?
- While we only see what's happening now, God looks at the long term. Do you need to become less shortsighted? How might looking at things through God's eyes help you today?

### SECRET BABY-SITTER

Baby Moses wasn't left to float alone in the water. Who was watching from nearby? (Exod. 2:4)

# Praying the Bible Together

Heavenly Father,

Thank You for watching over Baby Moses. I know you'll watch over me. Moses never forgot the feeling of Your arms around him when danger threatened. Thank You for the words Moses wrote when he was old: "The eternal God is your refuge, and underneath are the everlasting arms" (Deut. 33:27).

Help me to never forget who's watching over us every moment of the day. Thank You for these promises of Your care: "I have made you and I will carry you; I will sustain you and I will rescue you" (Isa. 46:4).

Thank You that You will never leave me or my family alone. You say: "I have summoned you by name; you are mine. When you pass through the waters, I will be with you; and when you pass through the rivers, they will not sweep over you" (Isa. 43:1-2).

I feel safe in Your arms today. Our whole family thanks You, Heavenly Father. We love You!

Amen.

**TRUTH TO GO**
God cares for me.
(1 Pet. 5:7)

# 78 | Playing Favorites

*The boys grew up, and Esau became a skillful hunter, a man of the open country, while Jacob was a quiet man, staying among the tents. [Their father] Isaac, who had a taste for wild game, loved Esau, but [their mother] Rebekah loved Jacob.*

GENESIS 25:27-28

Have you ever felt as if someone in the family was a favorite? You wanted that purple bike, but your brother got it instead? Your little sister always gets special treatment? That's what happened to the twin brothers Esau and Jacob. As they grew up, Mother favored Jacob, but Father's favorite was Esau.

One day the time had come for Isaac, who was old and nearly blind, to pass on his inheritance. It should have gone to the older twin, Esau. But with his mother's help, Jacob dressed up like Esau and tricked his father into giving it to him instead. As you can guess, that made Esau very angry. The two brothers remained enemies for twenty years.

### FAMILY TALK

↪ Why is playing favorites wrong?

↪ Does anyone have hurt feelings about this in your family? What can you do to make things more fair?

### DADDY'S BOY

Jacob didn't learn his lesson. When he had his own family, Jacob treated his next-to-youngest son as Daddy's favorite, and the other brothers hated him for it. Jacob made this son a special colorful coat. What was the boy's name? (Gen. 37:3-4)

# Praying the Bible Together

Heavenly Father,

Thank You that You love us all the same—and that each one of us is special to You too! Help us to treat each person in this family just like that!

The Bible says: "As believers in our glorious Lord Jesus Christ, don't show favoritism" (James 2:1).

You teach us that treating one person better than another is like setting ourselves up as a judge with evil thoughts (James 2:4). Instead, may we care about being fair.

The Bible says: "You are the body of Christ, and each one of you is a part of it" (1 Cor. 12:27).

Give us loyal love for each other, even when one of us is going through a stage when we're hard to get along with.

Help us to remember today: "How good and pleasant it is when brothers live together in unity.... There the Lord bestows his blessing" (Ps. 133:1,3).

That's the kind of family we're asking for, dear Lord.

Amen.

**TRUTH TO GO**
Everyone's special here.
(1 Cor. 12:27)

# 79 | You Can't Outgive God

*"Will a man rob God? Yet you rob me.... In tithes and offerings.... Bring the whole tithe into the storehouse, that there may be food in my house. Test me in this," says the LORD Almighty, "and see if I will not throw open the floodgates of heaven and pour out so much blessing that you will not have room enough for it."*

MALACHI 3:8-10

In the Bible a tithe actually means 10 percent. When you tithe, you give one-tenth of what you earn to God's work. But how much you give is not as important as your attitude about giving it. God wants us to *want* to give back to Him because He's given so much to us. In these verses we see how God feels about people who get stingy—He calls them robbers!

Giving is a way of saying thank You to God. And God has an amazing surprise in store for people who do give. He promises to give us so much in return that we won't have room to store all our blessings!

## FAMILY TALK

- Besides money, we can give time, work, or talents to God. How could your family become more generous—and more creative—in how you give?
- How does giving make you feel?
- Share a time when you gave to someone in need, then noticed that God gave something back to you in a special way.

## WHERE DOES IT GO?

God set up the practice of tithing to provide income and food for priests and their families. Name three ways our tithes are used today.

# Praying the Bible Together

Lord of all our resources,
> You give to us so generously.
> Why are we, in turn, sometimes so afraid to give to You?
> Forgive us when we get stingy.
> We receive Your advice to us today:

> > Give, and you will receive. You will be given much. It
> > will be poured into your hands—more than you can
> > hold. You will be given so much that it will spill into
> > your lap. The way you give to others is the way God
> > will give to you. (Luke 6:38, ICB)

Help us, Lord, to trust You enough to let You prove today that You
will provide for all our needs—and the needs of others through us!
Amen.

**TRUTH TO GO**
The more I give, the more I'll receive.
(Luke 6:38)

# 80 | God's Flashlight

*Your Word is a lamp to my feet and a light for my path.*

PSALM 119:105

When was the last time you used a flashlight? Were you camping? Had the electricity gone out at your house? Were you at a slumber party?

Think for just a minute about how you use a flashlight. If you want to see where you're going in the dark, you don't shine the light on your face. Or on your toes. Or behind you. You shine the light just enough in front of your feet so you can see the path. Then the light shows you where to walk.

God says the Bible works just like a flashlight or a lamp. If we'll turn it on (open the Bible and read), God's light will show us what to watch out for and where to step. We will be able to see what's right and good for us, and we won't get lost in the dark.

### FAMILY TALK

- The Bible uses other word pictures to describe what God's Word is like: honey (Ps. 119:103), fire and a hammer (Jer. 23:29), and a sword (Heb. 4:12). Make up your own word pictures, then explain how they show something important about what the Bible does for you when you read it.

- When did you last feel "lost in the dark"? Did God's Word help you see the light? How might it have if you'd "turned it on"?

### TURN ON THE LIGHT

Who said, "I am the light of the world"? (John 8:12)

# Praying the Bible Together

Dear Heavenly Father,
We each have a different direction to go today—school, jobs, homework, housework. Thank You that...

*Your Word will light our way!* (from Ps. 119:105).

So often when we try to see ahead in our lives, the road looks dark; we don't know what will happen. Thank You that...

*Your Word will light our way!*

We get upset because we can't see and figure it all out. Thank You that...

*Your Word will light our way!*

Help us to take Your teachings with us every day. Help us to open the Bible and read it, and think about it, and remember it, and do what it says. That's the only way...

*Your Word will light our way!*

Bring Your Word to our minds today when we need light most. Thank You for Your promise that no matter how dark things get...

*Your Word will light our way!*
Amen.

**TRUTH TO GO**
God's Word lights my way.
(Ps.119:105)

# 81 | What's on TV?

*Whatever is true, whatever is noble, whatever is right, whatever is pure, whatever is lovely, whatever is admirable—if anything is excellent or praiseworthy—think about such things.*

PHILIPPIANS 4:8

There's an old saying, "Garbage in, garbage out." It means that if you put bad thoughts and values into your mind, bad words and attitudes and actions will eventually come back out! But the opposite is true too: If your mind takes in "whatever is true, whatever is noble," you will have true and noble thoughts and actions.

This is why Paul told Christians to be sure to only think about good things. It's easy to forget that what we watch on TV, what we read, the friends we hang out with, and the music we listen to is "feeding" our thoughts and feelings. If it's "excellent and praiseworthy," we feel better. And our lives show it. But if it's garbage in, well…it's probably going to be garbage out!

### FAMILY TALK

- Can you name ways people are influenced negatively by TV, movies, or music? Is there "garbage" your family needs to dump?
- Pick one "excellent and praiseworthy" thing that you plan to think about a lot today (e.g., a Bible verse, something encouraging a person said, a Truth to Go from this book).

### HELLO THERE!

After Jesus rose from the dead, three times He greeted the disciples with the same good and "lovely" phrase. What was it? (John 20:19-27)

# Praying Psalm 101 Together

Dear Lord,

We praise You today for Your love and justice (v. 1). You are excellent and praiseworthy in every way! And we want to become more like You every day.

Help our family to lead a blameless life in what we talk about, how we spend our time, what we do for fun, and what we read and see (v. 2).

May we walk in our house every day with clean hearts. Help us to set no wrong thing or bad influence before our eyes or ears (v. 3). We never want to make heroes of anyone who stands for what You hate. Help us to have nothing to do with evil (v. 4).

When people gossip or make crass jokes, help us to turn away. When TV, radio, or movies celebrate proud, crude, or disrespectful behavior, help us to turn them off or make a better choice (v. 5). May any person or influence that glorifies lying or deception be kept outside our doors. Instead, help us to seek out and honor people who honor You and who can show us how to do the same (vv. 6-7).

Help us, Lord, to renew this resolution every morning:

Whatever is true, whatever is noble, whatever is right, whatever is pure, whatever is lovely, whatever is admirable—if anything is excellent or praiseworthy—we will think about such things (Phil. 4:8).

Amen.

**TRUTH TO GO**
If it's not excellent, it's not for me.
(Phil. 4:8)

# 82 | All Day Long

*Seven times a day I praise you for your righteous laws. Great peace have they who love your law and nothing can make them stumble.*

PSALM 119:164-165

Bet you've never heard Dad say, "Wow, I better remember to grow whiskers today!" Whiskers just grow on their own, without any reminders. But without a reminder some really important things don't happen. Like, "Ryan, remember your lunch money," or, "Shelley, did you send your thank-you notes yet?"

Most of us need reminders to praise God. It's easy to forget because we spend so much time thinking about ourselves. When you praise others, you think about *them* and talk about what great people they are. Praising God is important because every good thing comes from Him (James 1:17)! And praising God is good for you, too! The Bible says if you give God your praise, then He'll give You an awesome day!

### FAMILY TALK

- When might be the easiest time during the day to remember to give God praise? The hardest? What could you do to remember to praise God?
- The Bible often talks about giving the "sacrifice of praise" (Heb. 13:15). What does "sacrifice" mean? Why does a gift that costs you something mean more to the person you give it to?

### ROCK CONCERT

Once when His disciples were loudly praising Jesus, people told them to be quiet. But Jesus said, "If they keep quiet, the _____ will cry out." (Luke 19:40)

# Praying the Bible Together

Great and Wonderful God,

We do want to praise You seven times a day, because You deserve it!

When we get up, we'll praise You for making a new day. "This is the day the LORD has made; let us rejoice and be glad in it" (Ps. 118:24)!

At breakfast, we will praise You for taking care of our family's needs. "You open your hand and satisfy the desires of every living thing" (Ps. 145:16).

When we go to school, we'll praise You for giving us imagination and abilities. "I am fearfully and wonderfully made" (Ps.139:14).

Before we eat lunch, we'll praise You for giving us Your strength. "The God of Israel gives power and strength to his people" (Ps. 68:35).

When we're tired in the afternoon, we'll even praise You for our weakness. Because You said, "My grace is enough for you. When you are weak, my power is made perfect in you" (2 Cor. 12:9, NCV).

When we're together at dinner, we'll praise You for family and friends. "Sons [and daughters] are a heritage from the LORD" (Ps. 127:3).

At bedtime, we'll praise You for safe homes. "My people will live in peaceful dwelling places…in undisturbed places of rest" (Isa. 32:18).

Yes, Lord, we'll praise You at all times! "I will extol the LORD at all times; his praise will always be on my lips" (Ps. 34:1).

Amen.

**TRUTH TO GO**
Awesome days begin with praise.
(Ps. 119:164-165)

# 83 | The Giants vs. the Grasshoppers

*The LORD said to Moses, "Send some men to explore the land of Canaan, which I am giving to the Israelites."... "See what the land is like."... So they went up and explored the land.... They gave Moses this account: "We went into the land to which you sent us, and it does flow with milk and honey!"... Caleb [one of the explorers]...said, "We should go up and take possession of the land, for we can certainly do it." But the men who had gone up with him said, "We can't...they are stronger than we are.... All the people we saw there are of great size.... We seemed like grasshoppers in our own eyes."*

NUMBERS 13:1-33

These verses tell the story about a big contest the Israelites lost without even trying! In sports that's called a forfeit. If only one team shows up for a contest, they get to count it as a win. The absent opponent has to take a loss. God wanted to show the Israelites what a wonderful place the Promised Land was. He wanted them to be excited and happy, especially because He guaranteed that the land would be theirs. But instead of getting excited, the Israelites got scared. "We're not going to fight," they said. "Those guys are giants, and we feel like grasshoppers!" Score: Giants—1; Grasshoppers—0!

### FAMILY TALK

- Talk about a "giant" problem or challenge that makes you feel like a "grasshopper." How do you think God sees it?
- Are you more likely to respond like Caleb or the others?

### GIANT IN THE LAND

What was the name of the giant who frightened King Saul and his soldiers so much that they refused to fight? (1 Sam. 17)

# Praying the Bible Together

Dear Lord Jesus,

Thank You that You understand when we get afraid of big obstacles in our lives. But remind us that You are strong enough to help us face any problem.

You did not give us a Spirit that makes us afraid. You gave us a spirit of power and love and self-control (2 Tim. 1:7).

You tell us in the Bible:

> Do not fear, for I am with you; do not be dismayed, for
> I am your God. I will strengthen you and help you; I
> will uphold you with my righteous right hand.... For I
> am the LORD, your God, who takes hold of your right
> hand and says to you, Do not fear; I will help you.
> (Isa. 40:10,13)

That's why we can say with confidence, "The Lord is my helper; I will not be afraid. What can man do to me?" (Heb. 13:6).

Help us not miss out on the good things You want to give us today just because we get scared. With Your strength we're not grasshoppers—we're giants!

Amen.

**TRUTH TO GO**
God is my helper. I will not be afraid.
(Heb. 13:6)

# 84 | My Heart Hurts, Lord

*The LORD is close to the brokenhearted and saves those who are crushed in spirit.*

PSALM 34:18

The Bible teaches that God is omnipresent. That's a big word that means God exists everywhere at once. He lives on the other side of the universe—and He lives in your bedroom and hears the prayers you whisper into your pillow. What an amazing God He is!

God's presence matters the most when we're feeling a lot of sorrow or pain. That's when we really want a loving Heavenly Father to take care of us and give us comfort. And God wants you to know, "When you're hurting, I am very, very close!" In fact, the Bible calls our Heavenly Father "the God of *all* comfort" (2 Cor 1:3). That's how much He cares!

### FAMILY TALK

- Talk about a time in your family when things were so hard, you weren't sure if God cared anymore. Why does feeling pain make it hard for most of us to trust in God's love?
- Jesus was called "a man of sorrows" (Isa. 53:3). How can that help you feel closer to God when you are feeling sad?

### GOD'S TEARS

What's the shortest verse in the Bible? (John 11:35)

# Praying the Bible Together

Dear God,

You know that a deep hurt has come to our family. Our hearts feel broken and our spirits are crushed. We can't make sense of anything. Should we pray for a miracle? For peace? For understanding? All our longings lie open before You (Ps. 38:9). Out of the depths, we cry to You, Lord (Ps. 130:1).

Be close to us, Comforter, as You've promised. Intercede for each of us (Rom. 8:26-27). Thank You that You do draw near to us when we pray to You (Deut. 4:7; Ps. 145:18). Come quickly, Lord. You are our only hope (Ps. 40:17).

Because we believe in You, we cling to Your promises. We know that not one of the good promises You've given this family has ever failed (Josh. 23:14). You have said You will deliver us, and we trust You now (Ps. 34:19).

How we long for the day when You will release us from our sorrow so that we can come and go again with joy and peace (Isa. 55:12).

*I am close to the brokenhearted, and I save those who are crushed in spirit* (from Ps. 34:18). *My favor lasts for a lifetime; weeping may remain for a night, but rejoicing comes in the morning* (from Ps. 30:5).

Thank You, Lord.

Amen.

**TRUTH TO GO**

God cares about all my troubles.

(1 Pet. 5:7)

# 85 | Holy Temples

*Run away from sexual sin. Every other sin that a man does is outside his body. But the one who sins sexually sins against his own body. You should know that your body is a temple for the Holy Spirit.... You do not own yourselves. You were bought by God for a price. So honor God with your bodies.*

1 CORINTHIANS 6:18-20, ICB

No doubt about it—right from the moment of conception, a baby is either boy or girl, male or female. The difference is important to God. He thought making the sexes different was a terrific idea. Sexual attraction is God's idea too. It draws a man and a woman together toward marriage, which is the closest, most loving relationship on earth.

But God wants us to save being sexually active until we're married. That's when sharing our bodies is holy and blessed. Unfortunately, God's plans for sex aren't popular these days. Many think they can have sex without being married. But today's verses teach us that sexual sin is a terrible mistake. It's like stealing from God, from the person you'll be married to someday, *and* from yourself!

### FAMILY TALK

➤ If God is the "landlord" of His temple on earth—our bodies— how can each member of your family be a "good renter" of his/her sexuality, looks, health, and mind?

➤ Think of some ways you could "run away" from making a mistake about sex.

### "I'M OUTTA HERE!"

Which Bible character was in such a rush to run away from sexual sin that he left a woman holding his coat? (Gen. 39:10-12)

# Praying the Bible Together

Heavenly Father,

Today we pray that everyone in our family will care about purity in our thoughts and in our actions. Our bodies belong to You. Your Holy Spirit lives in us every day. Help us to honor You with how we treat our bodies (1 Cor. 6:18-20).

Thank You that You made us to be male and female and to be interested in sex (Gen. 1:27). But You want us to save sex for marriage (Heb. 13:4). Help our family to embrace healthy attitudes about our bodies and to show You respect by what we look at, by what we touch, by what we think about, and by how we behave around the opposite sex. Don't let us be fooled by the immoral values that are so common on TV or in the movies or at school. Purity *does* matter! Abstinence *is* cool—and the right thing to do! Refusing to tell dirty jokes or look at pornography *is* the mark of a very smart person!

Protect us from dangerous or immoral companions—people who use sex instead of guarding it. By Your Holy Spirit, show us when it's time to say, "Please don't do that," or "I have to go home now."

And when we face any kind of temptation, thank You that You will always help us if we ask and show us a way out (1 Cor. 10:13).

In Jesus' name we pray. Amen.

**TRUTH TO GO**
My body is a temple of the Holy Spirit.
(1 Cor. 6:19)

# 86 | Pants on Fire

*Do not lie to one another.*

Colossians 3:9, NASB

Maybe you've heard kids yelling, "Liar! Liar! Pants on fire! Hanging from a telephone wire!" Funny but true—when you tell a lie, you usually find yourself in bad trouble. You tell one lie—"I didn't break the lamp, Mom." But it leads to another one—"The dog knocked it over." Before you know it, you're trying to explain how the dog could reach a lamp that sits on a table four feet off the ground. Then if Mom doesn't believe you, you tell the biggest whopper of all—"What do you mean, you don't believe me? I would *never* lie to you!"

When Mom and Dad finally figure out that you're lying, you get in far more trouble than you would have if you'd just told the truth. And worst of all, you've lost their trust. From now on every word you say could be just another lie.

Jesus said, "Whoever can be trusted with very little can also be trusted with very much." If you want people to trust what you say when it is really important, then always tell the truth—no matter what!

### FAMILY TALK

- A friend you don't want to talk to calls. You tell your sister to say, "Allan's not here." Are these "white lies" wrong too? Why?
- When is it easiest for you to lie? What could you do to become more honest?

### KING OF WHOPPERS

Who does the Bible say is the "father of lies"? (John 8:44)

# Praying the Bible Together

Dear Lord Jesus,

You are the God of truth. You even said, "I am the truth" (John 14:6). Lord Jesus, we want to be like You, not like Satan, "the father of lies" (John 8:44). We want to make telling the truth a habit in our family. Please help us. We admit it's easy to lie, Lord. We just naturally respond in deceitful ways (Jer. 17:9). But You ask us to be truthful all the way through. Teach us wisdom in our deepest heart (Ps. 51:6).

Thank You for Your promise: "If you hold to my teaching, you are really my disciples. Then you will know the truth, and the truth will set you free" (John 8:31-32).

Please help us to stand up for honesty even when others don't. When friends cheat on tests, lie to their parents, or spread untrue rumors about kids they don't like, help us to choose to be truthful. Help us to tell the truth even when it hurts, because lying only makes more trouble and because Your Word says: "Truth will last forever. But lies last only a moment" and "The Lord hates those who tell lies. But he is pleased with those who do what they promise" (Prov. 12:19,22, ICB).

We pray in Jesus' name. Amen.

**TRUTH TO GO**
Do not lie!
(Col. 3:1)

# 87 | The Comeback Kid

*Jabez was more honorable than his brothers. His mother had named him Jabez, saying, "I gave birth to him in pain." Jabez cried out to the God of Israel, "Oh, that you would bless me and enlarge my territory! Let your hand be with me, and keep me from harm so that I will be free from pain." And God granted his request.*

1 CHRONICLES 4:9-10

Start reading 1 Chronicles out loud and see what happens! The first nine chapters are all just lists of names like "Dumah," "Zepho," and "Hazzobebah." All those unusual names will either give you mouth cramps or put you to sleep! But in the middle of chapter 4, you'll meet a man whose name not only sounds weird but means something weird too! He's Jabez, the man whose name means "pain."

How would you like to go through life with a name like that? "Hey, Pain! We don't want to play with you!" Or, "You know, Pain, you really are a *pain!*"

Jabez didn't want that either. Even though his life had started out all wrong, he decided to ask God to change his future. And God answered his request. By the end of his life, Jabez was everybody's hero, known far and wide for his honor and his success.

### FAMILY TALK

- Do you feel you face certain disadvantages? What are they?
- Read Jabez's life story again. Why do you think God answered his prayer?

### TOP NAME

Who has the "name that is above every name"? (Phil. 2:9)

# Praying the Bible Together

Dear Heavenly Father,

Thank You that we can always start over! We're not stuck because of what family we come from, or what name we have, or what mistakes we've made, or how far we've fallen behind. You invite us to reach for a comeback with Your strength.

Thank You for Your promise: *Forget what happened before. Do not think about the past. Look at the new thing I am going to do. It is already happening. Don't you see it?* (Isa. 43:18-19, ICB).

Today we pray with Jabez for a comeback.

"Oh, that You would bless us indeed!" We ask for Your special favor, Lord. Your blessing is our greatest wealth (Prov. 10:22, TLB)!

"Oh, that You would enlarge our territory!" Please, bring us greater success and more influence for You. Your Word says, "Delight yourself in the LORD and he will give you the desires of your heart" (Ps. 37:4).

"Oh, that You would keep Your hand upon us!" Give us Your mighty power, Lord, so we can overcome everything that holds us back. You promise us a Holy Spirit of power, love, and self-control (2 Tim. 1:7).

"Oh that You would keep us from harm!" Jesus taught us to pray, "Deliver us from evil" (Matt. 6:13). We're asking You to keep us safe.

Thank You for hearing our prayer, and answering our requests. Amen.

**TRUTH TO GO**
God wants me to be a Comeback Kid!
(1 Chron. 4:9-10)

# 88 | Nature Lessons

*The heavens tell the glory of God. And the skies announce what his hands have made. Day after day they tell the story. Night after night they tell it again. They have no speech or words. They don't make any sound to be heard. But their message goes out through all the world.*

PSALM 19:1-4, ICB

Have you ever been asked to prove the existence of God? Those who ask want an argument or a fact that makes God as obvious as the nose on their face.

The Bible says we have that proof. It's all around us in the created world. It's in the stars, in a butterfly's wing, in the sounds of a baby gurgling. Everything in the natural world is a miracle—proof that our Creator God is real! How could someone think a new house went up in your neighborhood without the help of a builder? How could anyone enjoy a painting without being sure that an artist had been at work? It's as obvious as the nose on your face!

The most important nature lesson you'll ever learn is this: *God, the creator, exists—and He is glorious!* The proof is all around you!

### FAMILY TALK

- Is there one miracle of nature that makes you think of God most of all (e.g., the ocean, a newborn baby, spring, a flower, the human hand)?
- Can you think of five things nature tells you about God?

### "HEY THERE, BIG DIPPER!"

"[The Lord] determines the number of the stars and calls them each by _____." (Ps. 147:4)

# Praying Psalm 8 Together

O Lord, our Lord,

How clearly we see Your presence and power in all the earth! And the wonder of You shines even brighter to our family than the wonder of Your creation (v. 1)!

You have created babies and children and parents to praise You. We want our words to join with the testimony of all creation so that doubters and sinners won't have any excuse for not believing in You (v. 2)!

When we look at the sun and the moon, the stars and the galaxies—all of them the works of Your hands—we're amazed that You care so much about us. You keep each one of us in Your mind at all times. Thank You (vv. 3-4)!

You made human beings to serve and worship only You. What a privilege and honor! Thank You for giving each person in this family important, meaningful work to do with our lives. We praise You (vv. 5-6)!

You ask us to take care of every kind of bird, animal, and fish (vv. 7-8). You ask us to be watchful and wise with the air, the water, the oceans, the mountains, the forests, and even the deserts. They're all miracles too.

O Lord, our Lord, how majestic is Your name in all the earth (v. 9)! Amen.

**TRUTH TO GO**
My Creator God exists—and He's amazing!
(Ps. 19:1)

# 89 | Grow Like This

*He is strong, like a tree planted by a river. It produces fruit in season. Its leaves don't die. Everything he does will be a success.*

PSALM 1:3, ICB

The Bible uses a lot of word pictures to illustrate what a good life looks like. Since the Israelites were farmers and animal keepers, a lot of the word pictures in the Bible are about plants and animals. One word picture that is common in the Bible is a healthy tree.

Imagine a beautiful tree with spreading branches and thick, green leaves. It's growing near a stream so it has lots of water. Its roots go down deep into the soil for nourishment. In its branches birds and hungry kids find plump, juicy fruit.

Get the picture?

**FAMILY TALK**

- A word picture can be explained in different ways, but it should help you understand something important. For the healthy tree in the verse, what could the water stand for? What about good soil? What about fruit?
- What could you do as a family to make sure you're trying to grow "strong, like a tree planted by a river"?

**TREE TALK**

Where was the "tree of the knowledge of good and evil" planted? (Gen. 2:15-17)

# Praying Psalm 1 Together

Dear Heavenly Father,

Thank You for showing us what a good life looks like. You want us to grow strong, and we want that too. Teach us from Psalm 1 today:

A good person doesn't listen to bad people, doesn't go where they go, or do what they do—and only a good person is truly happy (v. 1)! Help us every day to choose to be happy. Help us to stay away from the wrong crowd and never envy what they do or have.

A good person loves the Lord's teachings and tries to live by them day and night (v. 2). Give us a sincere desire to know the Bible and remember it.

A good person's life looks like a strong tree planted by a river. It produces fruit, doesn't die during a drought, and just keeps growing (v. 3). Lord, that's the kind of success we ask for! May we flourish in Your care and produce lots of fruit to bless others.

Thank You for showing us, too, Lord, what bad people look like. They dry up like weeds. They blow away like straw. And they'll never find the happiness they want. Instead, they'll end up being punished for their sins (vv. 4-5).

Thank You, Lord, for putting up a wall of blessing and protection around kids who choose to be good (v. 6). That's what we ask for today.

Amen.

**TRUTH TO GO**
I want to grow up good like a tree by a river.
(Ps. 1)

# 90 | Heaven, Our Home

*There are many rooms in my Father's house. I would not tell you this if it were not true. I am going there to prepare a place for you. After I go and prepare a place for you, I will come back. Then I will take you to be with me so that you may be where I am.*

JOHN 14:2-3, ICB

When Jesus was getting ready to go back to heaven, He wanted to tell His friends about where He was going. He didn't want them to feel left behind. He didn't want them to worry. And He didn't want them to be afraid of dying. So He told them good news about "my Father's house." That was Jesus' way of talking about heaven.

Today's verses tell us some very important things about heaven:
- Jesus hasn't forgotten about us or left us behind.
- Heaven is a wonderful place.
- Jesus is preparing a special place there for each of us.
- At the right time, Jesus will take us to heaven to live with Him.

God already knows exactly when we'll die—and how (Ps. 139:16). So we don't need to worry about it. And for Christians, death is just the beginning of the best part of life—spending eternity in heaven, our real home.

### FAMILY TALK

➤ What do you most look forward to in heaven?

➤ What questions do you plan to ask Jesus when you get there?

### NO MORE TEARS

When the apostle John saw a vision of the future, what did he notice about tears and crying in heaven? (Rev. 21:3-4)

# Praying the Bible Together

Dear Lord,

Thank You for Your promise of heaven! We can't wait to join You there someday.

Thank You that in Your home there's plenty of room for everyone (John 14:2). And You promise that when we get there, we will finally get to see You face to face (1 Cor. 13:12)!

We look forward to the day when we will all get new bodies, the kind that will last forever (2 Cor. 5:1). You say that heaven will be a place where there is no pain, no crying, no sadness, no night, and no death (Rev. 21:4). We praise You for this today, Jesus!

Thank You that we don't have to be afraid of dying. You promised:

*I am the resurrection and the life. He who believes in me will live, even though he dies* (John 11:25)

and,

*Whoever believes in the Son has eternal life* (John 3:36).

We love You, Lord, and we thank You for preparing a heavenly home just for us.

Amen.

**TRUTH TO GO**
Heaven is my Forever Home.
(John 14:2)

# Prayers for Special Times

# 1 | A Prayer for Healing

*While [Jesus] was by the lake...one of the synagogue rulers, named Jairus, came there. Seeing Jesus, he fell at his feet and pleaded earnestly with him, "My little daughter is dying. Please come and put your hands on her so that she will be healed and live." So Jesus went with him.*

MARK 5:21-24

Dear Lord,

We pray for _____ who is sick and needs your help. At times like these we feel so helpless! Please come to our home today, as You did to Jairus's house when You touched his little girl and made her well. Put Your hands on _____. You are the Great Physician (Luke 5:31).

Thank You for caring so much about our bodies and our health. You care about everything from sniffles to life-threatening diseases. Thank You that You spent so much time healing people when You were here on earth (Matt. 9:35). We know that you'll do the same for those we love.

With one touch, with one word, move with Your power even where our faith falls short (Mark 9:24 ). Bring strength and physical comfort to _____. Breathe out Your peace and rest. Bring patience, courage, and hope.

Hear our plea, Lord! Heal _____, and he/she shall be healed; rescue him/her, and _____ will be completely well (Jer. 17:14)! May he/she know beyond doubt that Your love is real—and ours is too!

In Jesus' name. Amen.

# 2 | A Prayer for Dedicating a Baby

*Hannah conceived and gave birth to a son. She named him Samuel, saying, "Because I asked the LORD for him."… She said to her husband, "After the boy is weaned, I will take him and present him before the LORD."*

1 SAMUEL 1:20,22

Lord of New Life,

Thank You for our baby, _____. What a miracle! What a blessing! You have shown our family Your love in a special way through this new life. And now as a sign of our worship we give our baby, _____, back into Your keeping.

We dedicate our baby to You, confident in Your steadfast faithfulness (2 Tim. 2:13). We vow to raise _____ according to Your ways and not our own, teaching him/her to seek You with all his/her heart (Deut. 4:29). We promise to do our best to write Your commandments on this child's heart (Deut. 6:7-8). And we ask You to help us always be patient and kind (1 Cor. 13:4).

Grant us Your wisdom to love and nurture this new being (James 1:5). May we always remember that he/she is a reward and a heritage from You, and not a burden (Ps. 127:3). Thank You for choosing us as the family for this precious child. We say with the psalmist:

> How can I repay the LORD for all his goodness to me? I will…call on the name of the LORD. I will fulfill my vows to the LORD in the presence of all his people. (Ps. 116:12-14)

In Jesus' name we pray. Amen.

# 3 | A Prayer from Psalm 5 for the First Day of School

*In the morning, O LORD, you hear my voice; in the morning I lay my requests before you and wait in expectation.*

PSALM 5:3

Gracious God,

On this first day of school, Lord, we all feel jitters, excitement, and a little fear. Hear my prayer this morning, Lord, on behalf of my precious children (v. 1). Thank You that I can lay my requests and worries before You each morning and wait in expectation (v. 3), for You are my King and my God (v. 2).

Remind my children each day ahead that certain behaviors and attitudes offend You: violence, rebellion, arrogance, and lying (vv. 4-6). May my kids take Your will to heart, and may they fear and reverence only You (v. 7).

When my children feel lost, make the way straight before them. Protect them from those who would harm them (vv. 8-10). Keep them safe from evil influences like drugs, profane talking and living, foolish values and foolish people, and every danger. Surround my children with a spiritual hedge of protection, and with friends and teachers who honor You (v. 12).

How glad I am, Lord, that You will help us. I will sing for joy as You spread protection over my children (v. 11). "For surely, O LORD, you bless the righteous; you surround them with your favor as with a shield" (v. 12).

I thank You and praise You.

Amen.

# 4. | A Graduation Prayer

*"For I know the plans I have for you," declares the LORD, "plans to prosper you and not harm you, plans to give you hope and a future. Then you will call upon me and come and pray to me, and I will listen to you. You will seek me and find me when you seek me with all your heart."*

JEREMIAH 29:11-13

Heavenly Father,

Today on this joyous occasion of _____'s graduation, we come to you as a family and commit his/her future into Your hands. You know how much we love _____ and how grateful we are that he/she has been part of our family all of these years. Even as we feel sadness at the thought of his/her growing up and leaving home, we rejoice in the good future we know You have in mind. For whether it is school, career, or a marriage partner someday, You alone can accomplish Your will in _____'s life. You alone can be faithful all his/her life to complete the good You began (Phil. 1:6).

Help _____ to remember that You have a plan. And that Your plan includes not only everyday concerns, but also what really counts—hope and a future (Jer. 29:11). When You say "hope," You don't just refer to an emotion, but something sure, solid—something worth living for. And when You say "future," You don't just mean that _____ will have a certain number of years ahead to live, but that the time will have great purpose.

Throughout the years ahead, we pray that _____ would call upon You and seek You with all his/her heart. For You have promised that You will hear, and You will be found (Jer. 29:12-13).

For all the decisions and challenges that lie ahead, may _____ seek You and live (Amos 5:4)! Thank You for Your promise that "he who pursues righteousness and love finds life, prosperity and honor" (Prov. 21:21).

For _____'s whole life, we claim these truths from Psalm 91:

- You will be _____'s true dwelling place and refuge (vv. 1-2).
- You will be a saving God under whose wings he/she can find covering and comfort (v. 4).
- You will save him/her from terrors and fears (v. 5).
- You will protect him/her from physical and spiritual diseases (v. 6).
- You will give Your angels power to guard _____ from evil persons or influences that want to bring harm (vv. 11-13).
- You will answer _____ when he/she calls to You for help, because You love him/her (v. 15).

Yes, Lord, You will always treasure _____, even more than we all do. We thank You and bless You today! And we commit _____ to Your loving care as he/she continues to grow into the beautiful person You created her/him to become.

Thank You, God!

Amen.

# 5 | A Prayer for a Child's Future Spouse

*The LORD God said, "It is not good for the man to be alone. I will make a helper suitable for him."*

Holy Lord,

In faith and hope, we intercede for the future spouse of _____. We pray that both _____ and his/her future spouse will make full and total commitments to You at a young age and that they will walk humbly with You, their God (Mic. 6:8). In every way, prepare these children for a godly marriage. May they grow up in all humility, considering others better than themselves (Phil. 2:3).

For this future new member of our family we pray for strong character, forged through perseverance (Rom. 5:4). May he/she grow to be a person of integrity, filled with and led by Your Spirit (Gal. 5:18). May he/she grow up to be rich in the fruit of the Spirit—love, joy, peace, patience, kindness, goodness, faithfulness, gentleness, and self-control (5:22-23). And we pray that _____ will please You with those traits too.

As these two children grow up, help them both to guard their purity because "marriage should be honored by all, and the marriage bed kept pure" (Heb. 13:4). We ask You these things because a godly spouse is a gift from You (Prov. 19:14).

Amen.

# 6 | A Birthday Prayer

*I pray that you, being rooted and established in love, may have power...to grasp how wide and long and high and deep is the love of Christ, and to know this love that surpasses knowledge—that you may be filled to the measure of all the fullness of God.*

EPHESIANS 3:17-19

Lord Jesus,

It is our joy and honor to pray for _____ on this special day. How grateful we are that You thought of making _____, and that from the moment of conception, You've been making him/her just exactly the way You wanted (Ps. 139:13)!

Today we pray that this child will celebrate this new year of life by reaching for Your best. Stand by him/her in every challenge. Bring light in every time of uncertainty. Thank You that You are able to make all grace abound to _____, so that in all things, at all times, having all that he/she needs, he/she will abound in every good work (2 Cor. 9:8).

Today, we claim Your mighty power and Your unfailing promises on behalf of _____. On this special day of cake and gifts and balloons, may he/she be able to grasp hold of the greatest gift of all—to know how wide and long and high and deep Your love really is (Eph. 3:19)!

In Jesus' name. Amen.

# 7 | An Easter Prayer

*The angel said to the women, "Do not be afraid, for I know that you are looking for Jesus, who was crucified. He is not here; he has risen, just as he said. Come and see the place where he lay. Then go quickly and tell his disciples: 'He has risen from the dead and is going ahead of you into Galilee. There you will see him.' Now I have told you."*

MATTHEW 28:5-7

O Risen Lord,
What a morning to love You! What a perfect day for happiness and hope and new beginnings!

*We celebrate You, risen Lord!*

You are the resurrection and the life. Thank You that every person in our family believes in You. Even though we will die in our bodies, we, too, will live eternally with You (John 11:25).

*We celebrate You, risen Lord!*

Thank You for defeating death and fear. Thank You for winning over Satan. Thank You for giving us the hope of heaven!

*We celebrate You, risen Lord!*

Since we've been raised to new life too, may we set our hearts on things above. As God's chosen people, may we treat everyone today with kindness, humility, gentleness, and patience (Col. 3:1,12).

That's how we'll keep celebrating You, risen Lord!
Amen.

# 8 | A Thanksgiving Day Prayer from Psalm 100

*Sing and make music in your heart to the Lord, always giving thanks to God the Father for everything, in the name of our Lord Jesus Christ.*

EPHESIANS 5:19-20

Heavenly Father,

Today as we celebrate Thanksgiving, we are grateful for food, friends, and family. We give You thanks, and we praise Your name. Together we say: *The LORD is good and his love endures forever* (v. 5).

We shout for joy to You, Lord! We want the whole world to know about how You take care of us all year long. We want to serve You gladly (vv. 1-2). We give You thanks, and we praise Your name, and together we say: *The LORD is good and his love endures forever.*

We *know* that You are God! You have made us, and we belong to You. We are Your people, and like sheep in Your pasture You keep us safe and cared for. We give thanks to You, and we praise Your name, and together we say: *The LORD is good and his love endures forever.*

Today we remember Your great love. We remember that You've been faithful in our yesterdays, and we're confident that You will be faithful in all our tomorrows. So we give thanks to You, and we praise Your name, and together we say: *The LORD is good and his love endures forever.*

Amen.

# 9 | A Christmas Prayer

*[The wise men] went on their way, and the star they had seen in the east*
*went ahead of them until it stopped over the place where the child was. When*
*they saw the star, they were overjoyed. On coming to the house, they saw the*
*child with his mother Mary, and they bowed down and worshiped him.*

Matthew 2:9-11

Heavenly Father,
This Christmas Day we come together
to thank You for Your greatest gift—
this baby in the manger, the only Son of God.
Happy Birthday, Jesus!
Thank You, Father, for loving the world so much
that You sent Your Son to be born
for our family
and for our world (John 3:16)!
Like the wise men and the shepherds,
we kneel before Jesus today with our gifts of love.
Like the angels we sing our carols of praise.
Like Mary and Joseph, we believe…
we believe…
and we are filled with Christmas joy!
Amen.

# 10 | A Parent's Blessing on a Child from Psalm 20

*The blessing of the LORD be upon you; we bless you in the name of the LORD.*

PSALM 129:8

The blessing of the Lord be upon you, _____.
    We bless you in the name of the Lord!
May the Lord answer you when you are in trouble.
May the name of our God protect you (v. 1).
May the Lord Himself send you help from His
    people, and His angels;
may He rescue You by His limitless power (v. 2).
May He remember the prayers you've said and the
    promises you've made.
May He accept your love and your sacrifices (v. 3).
_____, may the Lord give you the desires of your
    heart, and make all your plans succeed (v. 4).
We will shout for joy when you are victorious!
We will lift up our banners in the name of our God
    (v. 5)!
Because it is in Jesus' name that we bless you.
Amen.

# Indexes

# Title Index

Abba, Father . . . . . . . . . . . . . . . 136

All Day Long. . . . . . . . . . . . . . . 178

All Wet . . . . . . . . . . . . . . . . . . . 124

Angels Watching over Me. . . . . . . 142

Angels Welcome Here . . . . . . . . . . 50

Armor of God, The . . . . . . . . . . . . 82

Bad Company . . . . . . . . . . . . . . . . 64

Barn Full of Surprises, A. . . . . . . . 152

Battling Giants. . . . . . . . . . . . . . . 140

Big Race, The . . . . . . . . . . . . . . . . 48

Birthday Prayer, A . . . . . . . . . . . . 205

Born Again . . . . . . . . . . . . . . . . . 106

Bread of Life, The . . . . . . . . . . . . . 84

Champion Giver, A . . . . . . . . . . . . 24

Christmas Prayer, A . . . . . . . . . . . 208

Comeback Kid, The. . . . . . . . . . . 188

"Dear World..." . . . . . . . . . . . . . . 158

Dirty Feet . . . . . . . . . . . . . . . . . . 58

Donkey Talk . . . . . . . . . . . . . . . . 74

Dumb and Dumber. . . . . . . . . . . . 86

Easter Prayer, An . . . . . . . . . . . . . 206

Encouragement Spoken Here! . . . . 78

Everybody's Special Here . . . . . . . . 30

Family of Aliens, A. . . . . . . . . . . . . 46

Friends to the End . . . . . . . . . . . . 114

Giants vs. the Grasshoppers, The . . 180

Gift of Laughter, The. . . . . . . . . . . 38

"God Bless You!" . . . . . . . . . . . . . . 98

God of Hippos and Hailstones. . . . 16

God's Flashlight . . . . . . . . . . . . . . 174

Graduation Prayer, A . . . . . . . . . . 202

Grow Like This . . . . . . . . . . . . . . 192

Heaven, Our Home. . . . . . . . . . . . 194

"Help, I'm Sinking!". . . . . . . . . . . 112

Hiding Place, The . . . . . . . . . . . . 166

Holy Help . . . . . . . . . . . . . . . . . . 32

Holy Temples. . . . . . . . . . . . . . . . 184

Humble Outfit, A . . . . . . . . . . . . . 52

"I Promise!" . . . . . . . . . . . . . . . . . 104

In a World of Hurt . . . . . . . . . . . . 56

Jesus in the Mirror . . . . . . . . . . . . 162

Jesus Kind of Love, A. . . . . . . . . . . 20

Judas's Big Mistake. . . . . . . . . . . . 134

Just Like Stars . . . . . . . . . . . . . . . 120

Juvenile Delinquent . . . . . . . . . . . 146

Knock Knock. . . . . . . . . . . . . . . . 40

Listen Up! . . . . . . . . . . . . . . . . . . 128

Lord's Prayer, The. . . . . . . . . . . . . 118

Lying Lion. . . . . . . . . . . . . . . . . . 110

Miracle at the Door . . . . . . . . . . . 42

Mouth on Fire . . . . . . . . . . . . . . . 26

My Heart Hurts, Lord . . . . . . . . . 182

Nature Lessons. . . . . . . . . . . . . . . 190

Not Guilty! . . . . . . . . . . . . . . . . . 130

Oh No, Not Manna Again! . . . . . . 28

Okay, I'm Convinced! . . . . . . . . . 122

On with the Show!. . . . . . . . . . . . 138

Out of the Lion's Mouth . . . . . . . 144

Pants on Fire . . . . . . . . . . . . . . . . 186

Parent's Blessing on a Child from
     Psalm 20, A . . . . . . . . . . . . . 209
Pass the Salt, Please . . . . . . . . . . 132
People Pleasers? . . . . . . . . . . . . . . 72
Pep Talk. . . . . . . . . . . . . . . . . . 164
Playing Favorites . . . . . . . . . . . . 170
Praise the Lord! . . . . . . . . . . . . . 156
Prayer for a Child's Future
     Spouse, A . . . . . . . . . . . . . . 204
Prayer for Dedicating a Baby, A . . 200
Prayer for Healing, A . . . . . . . . . 199
Prayer from Psalm 5 for the First
     Day of School, A . . . . . . . . . 201
Right Place at the Right
     Time, The . . . . . . . . . . . . . . 94
Right Thing to Do, The. . . . . . . . 88
Second Chances. . . . . . . . . . . . . . 90
Somebody Important . . . . . . . . . . 108
Someone's Watching over You . . . 168
"Speak, Lord—I'm Listening..." . . 54
Shh...It's a Secret! . . . . . . . . . . . 66
Sterling Reputation, A . . . . . . . . . 36
Stop Fighting! . . . . . . . . . . . . . . 44
Sure Foundation, A . . . . . . . . . . . 76
Sweet as Honey . . . . . . . . . . . . . . 34
"Take It from Me" . . . . . . . . . . . . 68

Talk to God...Anytime,
     Anywhere . . . . . . . . . . . . . . 126
Ten to Keep, Part 1 . . . . . . . . . . 148
Ten to Keep, Part 2 . . . . . . . . . . 150
Testing, Testing... . . . . . . . . . . . 116
Thanks a Lot!. . . . . . . . . . . . . . . 60
Thanksgiving Day Prayer from
     Psalm 100, A . . . . . . . . . . . 207
There's a Frog in My Bed! There's a
     Frog on My Head! . . . . . . . . 22
Time for Church . . . . . . . . . . . . . 96
Two for the Road. . . . . . . . . . . . 160
Up a Tree. . . . . . . . . . . . . . . . . . 18
Veggies with Love. . . . . . . . . . . . 92
What's on TV?. . . . . . . . . . . . . . 176
When Bad Guys Go Good. . . . . . 102
Whose Turn for Dishes? . . . . . . . 154
Wonderful Shepherd . . . . . . . . . . 80
You Can't Outgive God . . . . . . . . 172
You Look Terrific! . . . . . . . . . . . . 70
"You'll Never Believe What
     I Heard!" . . . . . . . . . . . . . . . 62
"You're Good at That!". . . . . . . . 100

# Topical Index

**Lord, teach our family Your ways about...**

angels . . . . . . . . . . . .42, 50, 74, 142

church attendance . . . . . . . . . . . . .96

creation . . . . . . . . . . . . . . . .16, 190

forgiveness . . . . . . . . . . . . . . . . .134

freedom in Christ . . . . . . . . . . . .130

giving . . . . . . . . . . . . . . . . .24, 172

grace . . . . . . . . . . . . . . . . . . . . .130

holiness . . . . . . . . . . . . . . . .32, 184

praise . . . . . . . . . . . . . . . . .156, 178

prayer . . . . . . . . . . . . . . . .118, 126

repentance . . . . . . . . . . . . . .90, 134

salvation . . . . . . . .18, 102, 106, 130

Scripture . . . . . . . .34, 104, 166, 174

spiritual food . . . . . . . . . . . .84, 192

spiritual warfare . . . . . . . . . .82, 140

temptation . . . . . . . . . . . . . .82, 110

Ten Commandments, the . . .148, 150

tests . . . . . . . . . . . . . . . . .116, 144

tithing . . . . . . . . . . . . . . . . . . . .172

trials . . . . . . . . . . . . . . . . . .76, 124

**Lord, bless our family with...**

comfort in our

    heartache . . . . . . .160, 182, 194

confidence in Your love . . . . .70, 122

deliverance . . . . . . . .22, 82, 110, 140

friends . . . . . . . . . . . . . . . .64, 114

growth . . . . . . . . . . . . . . . .162, 192

guidance . . . . . . . . . . .68, 166, 174

peace . . . . . . . . . . . . . . . . . .44, 178

protection . . . . . . .80, 142, 168, 180

provision . . . . . . . . . . . . . .84, 172

Your affection . . . . . . . . . . . . . . .80

Your love . . . . . . . . . . . . . . . .20, 60

Your promises . . . . . . .104, 164, 194

Your voice . . . . . . . . . . . . . .54, 128

**Lord, keep this family from...**

arguments . . . . . . . . . . . . . . . . . .44

arrogance . . . . . . . . . . . . . . . . . .146

being people pleasers . . . . . . . .46, 72

betrayals . . . . . . . . . . . . . . . .66, 134

cheating . . . . . . . . . . . . . . . . . . .86

complaining . . . . . . . . . . .28, 92, 124

condemnation,

    feelings of . . . . . . . .78, 130, 188

conforming to the world . . . . . . . .46

discouragement . . . .48, 56, 160, 164

doubt . . . . . . . . . . . . . . . . .122, 190

favoritism . . . . . . . . . . . . . . .30, 170

fear . . . . . . . . . . . .80, 112, 140, 180

foolishness . . . . . . . . . . . . . . . . . .64

gossip . . . . . . . . . . . . . . . . . .26, 62

laziness . . . . . . . . . . . . . . . . . . . .154

lying . . . . . . . . . . . . . . . . . . . . .186

prejudice . . . . . . . . . . . . . . . . . .30

pride . . . . . . . . . . . . . . . .52, 58, 68

rebellion . . . . . . . . . . . . . . . . . . . .74

Satan . . . . . . . . . . . . . . . . . .82, 110

sin . . . . . . . . . . . . . . . . .48, 56, 184

stealing . . . . . . . . . . . . . . . . . . . .150

stubbornness . . . . . . . . . . . . . . . .74

wrong crowd, the . . . . . . . . . . . . . .64

**Lord, we give You thanks for...**

beauty . . . . . . . . . . . . . . . . . . . . . .70

being our Abba Father . . . . . . . . .136

choosing us . . . . . . . . . . . . . .94, 108

freedom . . . . . . . . . . . . . . . . . . . .22

heaven . . . . . . . . . . . . . . . . . . . . .194

hope . . . . . . . . . . .56, 164, 182, 188

laughter . . . . . . . . . . . . . . . . . . . .38

our friends . . . . . . . . . . . . . .64, 114

our home . . . . . . . . . . . . . . . . . . .76

our salvation . . . . . . . . . . .102, 106

second chances . . . . . . . . . . .90, 134

Your justice . . . . . . . . . . . . . . . . .144

Your miracles . . . . . . . . . . . . .60, 138

Your rest . . . . . . . . . . . . . . . . . . .32

Your surprises . . . . . . . . .42, 152, 160

Your ways . . . . . . . . . . . . . . . . . .152

Your Word . . . . . . .34, 104, 166, 174

**Lord, help our family to...**

be fair . . . . . . . . . . . . . . . . . . . . .170

be generous . . . . . . . . . . . . . .24, 172

be good . . . . . . . . . . . . . . . . . . . .32

be honest . . . . . . . . . . . . . . .72, 176

be hungry for You . . . . . . . . .84, 192

be lights . . . . . . . . . . . . . . .120, 158

be loyal . . . . . . . . . . . . . . . .66, 114

be obedient . . . . . . .76, 90, 148, 150

be patient . . . . . . . . . . . . . . . . . . .124

be thankful . . . . . . . .28, 60, 92, 156

be transformed . . . . . . . . . . . . . . .162

be wise . . . . . . . . . . . . . . . . .76, 146

be Your

    witnesses . .18, 46, 102, 120, 158

bless others . . . . . . . . . . . . . .50, 98

create harmony . . . . . . . . . . . .44, 92

encourage others . . . . . . . . . . .78, 98

have courage . . . . . . .112, 124, 180

have faith . . . . . . . . . . . . . .116, 190

have good

    conversations . . . . . .26, 62, 132

hear Your voice . . . . . . . . . . . . . . .54

help out . . . . . . . . . . . . . . . . . . . .154

honor our parents . . . . . . . . . . . . .88

keep good reputations . . . . . .36, 184

listen well . . . . . . . . . . . . . . .68, 128

love others . . . . . . . . . . . . . . . . . .20

make peace . . . . . . . . . . . . . . . . . .44

make the most of opportunities . . .94

memorize Your Word . . . . . . . . . .166

not discriminate . . . . . . . . . .30, 170

persevere . . . . . . . . . . .40, 110, 188

practice humility . . . . . . . . . . . . . .52

pray . . . . . . . .40, 42, 118, 126, 144

serve . . . . . . . . . . . . . . . . . .58, 100

show compassion . . . . . . . . . . . .182

show gratitude . . . . . . . . . . . .28, 60

show hospitality . . . . . . . . . . . . . .50

take advice . . . . . . . . . . . . . . . . . .68

trust You . . . . . . . . .16, 56, 124, 168

use our talents wisely . .100, 146, 172

use words wisely . . . . . . .26, 132, 186

value sexual purity . . . . . . . .146, 184

watch our tongue . . . . . . . . . . . . .26

welcome strangers . . . . . . . . . . . .50

**Bible Characters**

Abraham's faith is tested . . . . . . .116

Ananias and Sapphira try to

    cheat God . . . . . . . . . . . . . .86

Balaam's donkey talks . . . . . . . . . .74

Daniel and the lions' den . . . . . . .144

David slays Goliath . . . . . . . . . . .140

Delilah betrays Samson's secret . . . .66

Esther saves the Jews . . . . . . . . . .94

Jabez prays a special prayer . . . . . .188

Jesus and His miracles . . . . . . . . .138

Jesus heals ten lepers . . . . . . . . . .60

Jesus is the Good Shepherd . . . . . .80

Jesus on the road to Emmaus . . . .160

Jesus walks on water . . . . . . . . . .112

Jesus washes His disciples' feet . . . .58

Job is answered by God . . . . . . . . .16

Jonah and the big fish . . . . . . . . .90

Joseph and Mary in Bethlehem . .152

Judas betrays Jesus . . . . . . . . . . .134

Moses is adopted by a princess . . .168

Moses receives the Ten

    Commandments . . . . . . . . .148

Moses tells Pharaoh to let God's

    people go . . . . . . . . . . . . . . .22

Nicodemus comes to

    Jesus at night . . . . . . . . . . .106

Noah and his family aboard

    the ark . . . . . . . . . . . . . . . .124

Peter is freed from prison . . . . . . .42

Peter tries to walk on water . . . . .112

Samson is foolish . . . . . . . . .66, 146

Samuel listens to God . . . . . . . . . .54

Sarah laughs at an angel's news . . . .38

Saul is converted to Christ . . . . . .102

Zacchaeus invites Jesus to

    his home . . . . . . . . . . . . . . .18

# RICH FULFILLING PRAYERS—
## FOR EVERY ASPECT OF LIFE.

Shift your prayer life into high gear as you witness how to use God's words in Scripture to transform your prayers for your children, marriage, family, and your life.

WATERBROOK
PRESS

*www.waterbrookpress.com*

*Available in bookstores everywhere.*

Printed in the United States
by Baker & Taylor Publisher Services